How to Become a Technical Recruiter

By: Jonathan Kidder

"I wish I would have had this book when I was new to technical recruiting. The world of software and systems engineering has become so segmented, and it can be overwhelming trying to grasp programming concepts. This book provides a foundational framework for understanding and sourcing all of the major IT roles." — Erin Mathew, Talent Sourcing Manager

"Jonathan has compiled a solid range of useful resources on a range of topics related to technical recruiting and sourcing. You'll particularly find valuable all the annotated descriptions of niche technical sites to find talent and related sample search strings, which are well targeted to common talent needs. Ditto for the detailed overviews of powerful search tools to source technical talent. Also useful are the overviews of each technical job role and sample screening questions for corresponding candidates and little extras sprinkled throughout, such as ways to tap talent from layoffs." — Glen Gutmacher VP Global Talent Sourcing

"How to Become a Technical Recruiter is a must-read book for anyone that is new to technical hiring. It provides both the foundational knowledge and high-level strategies to successfully hire technical talent at any organization." — Jeese Tinsley Senior Recruiter

"This is the most comprehensive book that I've read that covers technical recruiting. Jonathan has clearly defined every major tech role, giving examples of how to phone screen and recruit the best talent online. Overall, I couldn't put this book down!" — Brian Fink Senior Recruiter Twitter

"Whether you are an experienced tech recruiter or you are just getting started, this is a must read! A brilliant explanation of tech stack, tools, techniques, and so much more. Not only will you stand out from the crowd, you will have success in making amazing tech hires." — Angie Verros Founder of Vaia Talent

"The explanation of the job is very important to understanding your search and to make it about the role, not just checking the box on programming language. This book is definitely a tool that every technical recruiter should have in their toolbox in order to be much more efficient and engaging!" — Michael Crouse, Senior Global Talent Acquisition Manager

"Very thorough take on how to understand and hire technical roles. This book takes the time to outline the research tools, jobs titles, functions, interview questions, search strings, candidate sites, email engagement, and campaigns used. If you need a "go-to" book on tech recruiting / sourcing, then this is it!" --
Mark Tortorici, SourceCon Editor

Legal Disclaimer

This book highlights different ways to find and recruit tech candidates for your job openings online. Please consult your Country's HR compliance in regards to recruiting. This includes understanding GDPR and OFCCP employment compliance. Discretion is advised before doing any of the suggestions listed in this book.

Table of Contents

A Guide to Technical Recruiting

This book was written to help turn the generalist recruiter into a Technical Recruiter. The Information Technology field can be intimidating for Recruiters. This book helps to clearly define the top Tech Jobs within the industry.

You will understand each skill requirement in every area within a role, understand additional search terms, improve your job description, and gain confidence when you assess a candidate's skills over a technical phone screen call.

This book will help give a Recruiter the core requirements and high-level overview of the top most common tech jobs.

The author of this book has almost over a decade of research talent sourcing experience within the technology space. Jonathan Kidder has trained Sourcers across the globe, and he's an active blogger within the community. He launched his blog WizardSourcer.com in 2015 which focuses on helping others learn about the latest talent sourcing tools.

He's excited to share the latest Boolean strings and recruitment tools on the market, and even more so, he's excited to help you on your journey of becoming a Wizard at talent sourcing.

Once this book was published in 2021, the tool, string, and websites suggestions were already out of date. Technology moves fast within the recruiting space. There will always be a newer & better tool out in the market. I wanted to highlight tools that have been tried and true for a while. The book will focus on core job categories that Recruiters and Sourcers will need to master in order to become a technical screener.

About Jonathan Kidder

Jonathan Kidder, AKA the "WizardSourcer," is a top-ranked technical talent sourcing recruiter, staffing expert, and corporate trainer who assists organizations of all sizes in identifying and attracting top talent.

A wizard at harnessing the power of social networking, Boolean strings, search aggregators, deep web searching, scrapers, and other advanced technology tricks and tools. In 2015, he founded a recruiting blog called WizardSourcer. Which has become one of leading knowledge resources for recruiters online.

His mission is simple: To help Recruiters understand Technical Roles.

With over a decade of full-cycle recruiting and sourcing experience under his belt, he has worked in talent sourcing and recruiting with companies including Amazon, Vista Outdoor, CA Technologies, American Express, and many others.

Throughout his career as a sourcing leader, he has pursued continuous learning to stay current on the latest sourcing trends and to help clients across industries maximize the use of high-tech recruiting tools ranging from browser extensions to AI automation.

After earning a bachelor's in business from Bethel University in Saint Paul, Minnesota, Jonathan launched his sourcing career at Allegis Global Solutions, one of the largest RPO staffing companies in the world.

At Allegis, Jonathan discovered the power of social media as a recruiting tool. This inspired him to develop and implement a proprietary employer branding EVP and recruitment marketing plan that could be used with any client to attract the world's best available talent.

A sought-after speaker and mentor, Jonathan has trained teams around the globe on best practices for sourcing and recruiting top talent. One of the industry's emerging go-to resources on recruiting expertise in the 21st century, he writes regularly on the latest recruiting trends for his own top-ranked blog at WizardSourcer in addition to being a contributing writer for AI recruiting platform Hiretual and Recruitingblogs.com.

He is the author of LinkedIn Revealed, Top Talent Sourcing Tools, & A Guide to Diversity Talent Sourcing. He currently lives in Minneapolis with his wife and adopted golden doodle named Henry.

Chapter 1: Defining Tech Roles

In this chapter, I will:
- Define each Technical Role
- Summarize the Jobs Description
- Explain Job Requirements
- Phone Screening Questions

Technology acronyms will no longer be intimidating, and you will be able to analyze a candidate's tech skills with confidence. Written in clear and concise prose, each job title defined with searchable keywords and phone screening questions will help turn the generalist recruiter into a confident technical recruiter.

Tech Talent is a phrase used to describe the highly sought-after workforce with the skills to drive growth and innovation at technology companies. This could include a wide variety of roles including IT professionals, computer science professionals, software developers, engineers, data scientists, and many more emerging positions.

Why are people needed in the technology industry? When the need for highly specialized labor combines with rapid evolution and growth—like in the tech industry—the skilled professionals who can fill those roles naturally experience high demand. In fact, research by Korn Ferry estimates that the labor skills shortage in the tech sector could reach as high as 4.3 million workers in 2030.

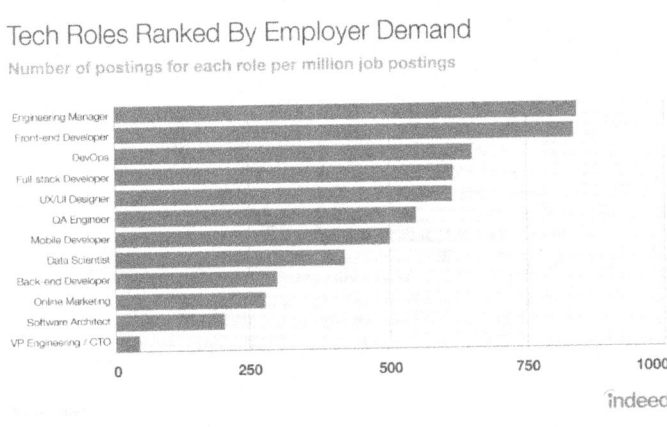

(Source: Indeed.com)

IT Roles: An Overview

So, we know that demand for tech talent is on the rise—and that leaves quite a bit of work for recruiters to catch up on.

With so many potential career paths available in the field, it can be daunting for recruiters to consider taking on a job in the tech industry. Fortunately, all it takes is a little research (and studying) to expand your IT knowledge.

To get you started, here is a brief overview of every IT role you're likely to come across (don't worry — we'll go over these in detail later).

Software Engineers:

Web Developers
Build and maintain websites, overseeing factors such as content, visuals, and more. Emphasis on design.

Frontend Developers
Build and maintain the front-end section of websites and/or applications (i.e., what visitors see and interact with). Emphasis on functionality.

Backend Developers
Build and maintain the servers of websites and applications by troubleshooting, debugging, optimizing, and more. Emphasis on maintenance.

Full Stack Developers
Oversee frontend and backend development tasks, possibly including UI/UX management, graphic design, building servers, etc.

Mobile App Developers
Develop mobile solutions for native and Swift-platform apps, working with tools like Java and JavaScript.

Desktop App Developers
Develop software applications for operating systems like macOS and Windows.

Analysts: Analyze data from their operation's business or technical side — or both.

AI & ML Specialists: Work with "Artificial Intelligence" and "Machine Learning" to craft intelligent algorithms.

Managers: Coordinate and lead their workforce's efforts to achieve specific goals, ranging across technical, product, engineering, and developmental departments

Designers: Oversee tasks like UX/UI creation, user research, and web design with a focus on visuals and/or functionality.

Infrastructure & Networking Specialists: Maintain, configure, and/or analyze technological infrastructure & networking systems for optimization.

Cloud Specialists: Utilize cloud technology to migrate services and information to the cloud.

Architects: Design, implement, evaluate, and manage technology systems in areas like software and security.

Cyber Security Specialists: Keep sensitive organizational data secure from threats like unauthorized access (both internal and external) and cybercrime.

Support Specialists: Work with external customers, internal clients, or employees to troubleshoot and solve technology issues.

Administrators: Oversee daily operations to maintain the organization's security systems, servers, and IT network.

Testing & QA Roles: "Test" software throughout its development to find bugs & issues and determine its functionality/quality.

Executives: Oversee the organization's IT development and management from a senior-level status.

Data & Business Intelligence Specialists: Provide the organization with software and tech tools designed to improve its output and efficacy.

Terms & Acronyms to Know

Whether you're in your early stages of job research or already have your foot in the door, some of the following terms will follow you everywhere. As such, it's a good idea to get familiarized with their basic definitions.

Terms:

Team Structure
- Matrix team, Agile team, Cross-functional team

Software Project
- Team Roles
  - Project Manager, Business Analyst, QA Manager

Technical Stack
- Application
- Server
  - Web server
  - Database server
- Operating System (OS)
- LAMP (Linux, Apache, MySQL, PHP)
- MEAN (MongoDB, Express.js, Angular, Node.js)
- MERN (MongoDB, Express.js, React, Node.js)

Software Development
- Process
  - Traditional Waterfall methodology
  - Test-Driven Development (TDD)
  - Agile methodologies
    - ⇒ eXtreme Programming (XP)
    - ⇒ Scrum

- - Product Owner
  - Scrum Master
  - Daily stand-up
  - Sprint
  - ⇒ Kanban
    - Kanban board
- Programming Language
  - Java
  - JavaScript
  - C#
  - PHP
  - Python
  - Ruby
  - C or C++
- Query language
  - SQL
- Procedural language
  - PL/SQL
  - COBOL
  - Fortran
- Markup language
  - HTML
  - XML
- Software framework
  - Ex: React, Angular, …
- Software library
- Three IT layers
  - Frontend (user-facing
  - Backend (server-side)
  - Storage (database)
- Design patterns
- Team roles

- o Frontend developer
- o Backend developer
- o Full-stack developer

Mobile Applications
- Android
  - o Java language
  - o Kotlin language
- iOS
  - o Objective-C language
  - o Swift language

Cloud Service Providers
- Amazon
  - o Amazon Web Services
- Google
  - o Google Cloud Platform
- Microsoft
  - o Microsoft Azure
- IBM
  - o IBM Cloud
- Oracle
  - o Oracle Cloud

Data
- Databases
  - o Relational
    - ⇒ MySQL
    - ⇒ MSSQL
    - ⇒ PostgreSQL
    - ⇒ Oracle
  - o Non-relational
  - o MongoDB

- Search engines
  - Elasticsearch
- Big Data
  - In the cloud
    - ⇒ Google BigQuery
    - ⇒ Amazon Elastic MapReduce (EMR)
    - ⇒ Oracle Big Data Cloud
  - On premise
    - ⇒ Hadoop
    - ⇒ Apache Spark

Testing
- Manual testing
- Automated testing
  - Frameworks (i.e., Selenium)
- Quality Assurance (QA)
- Functional testing
  - Sanity testing
  - Regression testing
- Non-functional testing
  - Security testing
  - Performance testing

DevOps
- Dev + Ops + QA

Product Prototyping
- MVP
- Design Sprint
- Software prototype

Design
- UX design
- UI design

Content Management Systems (CMS)
- Wordpress
- Drupal
- Joomla
- Magento

Software Code Repositories
- Technology
  - Git
  - SVN (legacy)
- Cloud providers (SaaS)
  - GitHub
  - GitLab
  - Bitbucket

Acronyms:

API
- Application Programming Interface

ASP
- Application Service Provider (SaaS provider)
- Active Server Pages

AWS
- Amazon Web Services

CI

- Continuous Integration

CD
- Continuous Delivery

CDN
- Content Delivery Network

CMS
- Continuous Management System

CSS
- Cascading Style Sheets

CX
- Customer Experience

DBMS
- Database Management System

GCP
- Google Cloud Platform

HTML
- Hyper-Text Markup Language

HTTP
- Hyper-Text Transfer Protocol

IaaS
- Infrastructure as a Service

IDE
- Integrated Development Environment

JEE
- Java Enterprise Edition
- Jakarta Enterprise Edition

J2EE
- Java 2 Platform, Enterprise Edition (legacy name)

J2SE
- Java 2 Platform, Standard Edition (legacy name)

JS
- Java Script

JSE
- Java Platform, Standard Edition (Java SE)

JSF
- JavaServer Faces

JSON
- JavaScript Object Notation

JSP
- JavaServer Pages

LAMP
- Linux, Apache, MySQL, PHP

MEAN

- MongoDB, Express.js, Angular, Node.js

MERN

- MongoDB, Express.js, React, Node.js

MS

- Microsoft (MS Windows, MS Azure)

MVP

- Minimum Viable Product

OOP

- Object Oriented Programming

OS

- Operating System (iOS, OS X, macOS)

PaaS

- Platform as a Service

PEAR

- PHP Extension and Application Repository

PHP

- Recursive acronym for "PHP: Hypertext Preprocessor"

PL/SQL

- Procedural Language SQL

REST
- Representational State Transfer

QA
- Quality Assurance

SAAS
- Software as a Service
- Storage as a Service
- Security as a Service

SDK
- Software Development KIT

SDLC
- Software Development Kit

SEO
- Search Engine Optimization

SLA
- Software License Agreement
- Service Level Agreement

SOAP
- Simple Object Access Protocol

SPA
- Simple Object Access Protocol

SQL
- Structured Query Language (MySQL, NoSQL)

SVN
- Subversion

UI
- User Interface

UX
- User Experience

XML
- Extensible Markup Language

IT Roles: In-depth

Now that we have a foundation laid, it's time to start building out the rest of your IT knowledge. In this next section, we'll take a deeper dive into some of the major roles found in the field.

1. Software Engineer

Software engineering is a field that is important to the IT industry. Software engineers work in collaboration with designers, data scientists, and project managers to figure out how to best create and support their processes and projects. They're also generally in charge of reviewing other people's code, meeting with team members, and doing a healthy amount of research.

Software engineers are more likely to work on computer systems as a whole. They develop standalone programs and apps to help users perform various activities. For the most part, they program, document, test, and maintain software by utilizing the best practices. Software engineers are required to have deep knowledge in different technologies some of them are: Java, C and C++, Python, C#, JavaScript and many more, depending on their engineering and developing purposes. There are different methodologies worth mentioning, like Scrum, Agile, and Kanban which are really important in the process of software development and automation.

Some crucial skills & knowledge those in the category should be able to present (according to their role) include:

Web Developers
- Website building
  - Wix
  - Square
- CMS
  - Wordpress
  - Joomla
  - Drupal

Frontend Developers
- Programming Language
  - JavaScript
- Software Framework

- React
- Angular
- Vue.js

Backend Developers
- Backend JavaScript development
  - Programming Language
    - JavaScript
  - Software Framework
    - Node.js
- Backend Python development
  - Programming Language
    - Python
  - Software Framework
    - Django
- Backend Java development
  - Programming Language
    - Java
  - Software Framework
    - Spring
    - Hibernate
- Backend PHP development
  - Programming Language
    - Java
  - Software Framework
    - Spring
    - Hibernate
- Backend C# development
  - Programming Language
    - C#
  - Software Framework
    - .NET Framework

- .NET Core
- Backend Ruby development
    - Programming Language
        - Ruby
    - Software Framework
        - Ruby on Rails
- Backend Perl development
    - Programming Language
    - Software Framework

Mobile App Developers
- Native apps
    - iOS app development
        - Objective-C
        - Swift
    - Android app development
        - Java
        - Kotlin
- Cross-platform apps
    - JavaScript
        - React Native
        - Ionic
        - Titanium Appcelerator
    - C#
        - Xamarin
    - Dark
        - Flutter

Desktop App Developers
- Application development
- Java development
    - JSE

Most software engineers will either work as full-time or short-term (freelance or internship contract) employees. You'll also find that most of them share the same interests, which we can split into four areas.

1. **Technical Stack**
   a. Obtaining must-have skills
   b. Having the option to upskill

2. **Work Methodology**
   a. SW dev methodology
   b. Cloud infrastructure
   c. Issue tracking
   d. DevOps setup
   e. Following best practices

3. **Teamwork**
   a. Knowing team size
   b. Identifying seniority levels
   c. Determining leaders and A-players

4. **Projects**
   a. Outlining project scopes

Though they may share similar interests, software engineers don't always operate the same way. Like most people, those in the field may follow a different path than their counterparts. But, from a recruiter standpoint, it's most effective to split these into common "personas" you're likely to encounter.

Maker vs. Crafter
- Makers overemphasize building and move from project to project without refining their code.
- Crafters use their high coding standards to edit, polish, and perfect production systems before moving to the next.

Builder vs. Maintainer
- Builders prefer to create new services, products, and technologies.
- Maintainers would rather oversee existing software to keep it in running smoothly.

All-rounder vs. Specialist
- All-rounders (or Generalists) understand a wide range of technologies, yet their knowledge is often surface level.
- Specialists narrow down to one specific technology to perfect their expertise.

Now, employees aren't the only ones with different personality traits. Much like the candidates they hire, different companies and teams will present unique advantages—and disadvantages—that can greatly impact their "fit" for an applicant. In the IT field, this comes down to four main categories.

Startups
These organizations are known to be flashy, tempting opportunities for candidates thanks to

their high opportunity for growth. As a newer team, many roles will be available for the taking.

Agencies

A company that provides technological solutions to clients, agencies often have a large variety of projects for employees to work on, possibly making it a more exciting environment.

Corporations

Those giant downtown skyscrapers are often home to mega corporations—many of which can't operate without a tech department. In most cases, candidates can look forward to more stability, comfort, and a potentially larger paycheck.

Product-centric Companies

With a deep emphasis on technology, these companies focus primarily on product development and customer satisfaction. Employment often includes various opportunities for growth and getting hands-on with multiple technologies.

Software engineering candidates will also need to have a good understanding of the software development process before entering the job market. Depending on their chosen methodology, this will follow one of the lifecycles below.

Development Stages:

1. Planning

2. Analysis
3. Design
4. Implementation
5. Maintenance

Project Management Methodologies:

Traditional Waterfall Method

1. Analyzing business requirements
2. Designing the system
3. Developing the software code
4. Testing the software code with user-acceptance tests
5. Deploying the software code
6. Maintaining the software code

Lean Method (Waste Reduction)

- Eliminates unnecessary work
- Limits excess materials
- Prevents quality defects
- Reduces backlog lengths
- Avoids overproduction

Agile Method

- 4 values
    - Individuals and interactions OVER process and tools
    - Working software OVER comprehensive documentation

- - Customer collaboration OVER contract negotiation
  - Responding to change OVER following a plan

- 12 Principles
  - Changing requirements are welcomed
  - Software is frequently delivered
  - Businesspeople & developers cooperate daily
  - Progress is measured through software efficacy
  - Teams are self-organizing
  - Reflection & adaptation occurs regularly
  - Customer satisfaction is measured through consistent software delivery
  - Teams display mutual support, trust, and motivation
  - Face-to-face interactions are emphasized
  - Processes should support repetition and a consistent development pace
  - Attention should be paid to design and technical detail
  - Simplicity is key

- 2 Methodologies
  - Scrum
    - Development is achieved through multiple implements

- Each section of development is completed in a "sprint"
- Scrum Teams, Masters, and Owners oversee progress
  - Kanban
    - Development is tracked and measured on a physical or virtual board
    - Tasks are standardized as "To Do," "In Progress," or "Done"
    - Emphasis placed on real-time communication and transparency

Again, since this field can cover quite a few bases, most roles will have developers focus on a specific area within software engineering. Each of these developmental niches require engineers to deal with "languages" regularly, which is the computer language they use to code (and the stuff that looks like gibberish to us normal folk).

As such, it's a good idea for recruiters to brush up on their understanding of coding language. Some jobs could require an engineer to have mastery of one or more specific languages, which can help recruiters filter out candidates easily.

Frontend Developer (User-facing)
- Development written in JavaScript language using...
  - Angular

- React

  OR

- Written in HTML

Backend Developer (Server-side)

- Written in JavaScript language using Node.js runtime environment

  OR

- Written in PHP language using...
  - Laravel
  - Symfony
  - Zend
- Written in C# language using...
  - .NET Framework
  - .NET Core

  OR

- Written in Java language using...
  - Spring
  - JSF

  OR

- Written in Ruby language using...
  - Ruby on Rails

  OR

- Written in Python language

Mobile Applications

- Native development for:
  - iOS using...
    - Objective-C language
    - Swift language
  - Android using...
    - Java language

- Kotlin language

OR

- Cross-platform development written in:
  - JavaScript language using React Native
  - C# Language using Xamarin
  - Dart language using Flutter

Usual software engineering search terms you can use for your recruiting purposes can be: software engineer, Java programmer/developer, C/C++ programmer, object-oriented programmer, Scrum master, etc.

Screening questions based on requirements:

Q: What programming languages are best to use?
A: It's always a good idea when the candidate has experience with C++ and with Java and has a willingness to operate with a new language. Python is a highly recommended language here, as well as JavaScript and its frameworks. Having an experience with Perl is a big plus too.

Q: What is the process of software developing, starting from requirements to delivery?
A: It is a complex life cycle with a structure applied to the development of a software product. There are several models for such processes including agile methods, which is crucial for getting clear requirements from the client and serving the best possible results.

Q: How to test your software and handle errors?
A: There are different software testing tools and practices for handling and locating errors. One of them is JUnit, which allows software testing part by part and easier error fixing than usual.

Pro Tip: Check out StackShare.io to see the tech stack of most major Tech companies within North America.

2. Software Manager

A software manager is a professional who is responsible for managing the software development process within an organization. They lead a team of software developers and engineers to develop, test, and deploy software solutions that meet business needs.

The role of a software manager is to ensure that software projects are completed on time, within budget, and to the required quality standards. They work with other departments, such as product management and quality assurance, to understand business needs and ensure that software development aligns with these needs.

Software managers typically have a strong background in software development and may have experience in specific programming languages or technologies. They must also have excellent leadership, communication, and project management skills to lead and motivate their teams to deliver high-quality software solutions.

The day-to-day tasks of a software manager may include assigning tasks to team members, setting deadlines, conducting code reviews, and working with other departments to identify and resolve software-related issues. They may also be responsible for overseeing the development of project budgets and schedules, and for reporting progress and status to upper management.

This role involves:
- Managing a team of people
- Leading the construction and design of systems
- Being responsible for the health of a set of systems
- Overseeing the production roadmap
- Assigning business and technical requirements to team members
- Managing the understanding, sizing, and scheduling of requirements
- Providing regular updates on the progress of development.

Keywords
- Software Developer, Technical Lead, leadership
- People Manager or People management
- Object Oriented Design Patterns
- System Design

- Distributed Systems, Distributed Computing
- Architecture, Architecture Design, Data Structures
- Code Reviews, Design Reviews
- Data Driven
- Scalable, Security, Latency, refactoring
- Cross-functional
- Technical Design
- Hiring, interviewing, career development

3. Technical Program Manager

A Technical Program Manager is a professional who manages complex technical projects from inception to completion. They use their expertise in project management, engineering, and technology to ensure that projects are delivered on time, within budget, and to the required quality standards.

The role of a Technical Program Manager involves working with cross-functional teams, including engineers, product managers, and business stakeholders, to identify business requirements and develop technical solutions that meet those requirements. They must be able to communicate effectively with technical and non-technical stakeholders, and have excellent leadership and project management skills.

Technical Program Managers are responsible for developing project plans, identifying project risks, and monitoring progress against established timelines and budgets. They must be able to make trade-offs between conflicting priorities and manage stakeholder expectations.

In addition to project management skills, Technical Program Managers must have a strong technical background and be able to understand complex technical systems and architecture. They may be required to provide technical guidance to their team members and work closely with software engineers and other technical professionals.

This role involves:
- Translating business requirements into detailed technical specifications for implementation by technical teams
- Coordinating, prioritizing, and reporting on the design, development, testing, and deployment of features
- Creating and tracking project milestones, risks, and dependencies
- Understanding design details and expectations for system dependencies
- Serving as the technical team's point of contact to address questions, clarify requirements, and provide feedback on features, timing, and implementation plans
- Taking responsibility for the implementation plan across multiple teams.

Areas of overlap:

- Stakeholder engagement (cross-team, cross-functional)
- Product Roadmap and Priorities
- Project Management
- Software Design and Construction

4. Product Manager Team (PMT)

A PMT, or Product Management Team, is responsible for overseeing the entire lifecycle of a product or feature, from its initial vision and roadmap to managing the business aspects of the product, such as branding, pricing, and public relations. They are also responsible for tracking key performance indicators (KPIs) and measuring the success of the product in the market.

In essence, PMTs are responsible for launching products or features into the market and ensuring their success by overseeing all aspects of their development, launch, and post-launch performance.

This role involves:
- Own the lifecycle of a product/feature
- Voice of the product's customer and are accountable for the customer's experience
- Own the product roadmap, vision, and tenets
- Manage the business of the product (e.g. branding/placement, economic modeling, pricing, forecast analysis, promotions, marketing, driving segment adoption, PR,

training sales, etc.), and reporting (e.g., KPIs, adoption, other measures of success)
- Manage the timelines for all associated software and services, supporting the launch of new releases

Keywords
- Product Definition/product strategy
- Pricing
- Feature/Roadmap Tradeoffs/Program Delivery/ Product Portfolio/product adoption
- system performance latency
- probe feature design choices
- product's performance
- technology trade-offs
- Product prioritization
- product design decisions
- scalability, future innovations
- Go to market strategy
- Technical depth
- Product management
- Enterprise product experience
- Content strategy
- Revenue goals
- escalation management
- Nice to have: MBA Degree

5. Front-End Developer
Front-end web development, also known as client-side development is the practice of producing HTML, CSS and JavaScript for a website or web application, so that a user can see and interact with

them directly. The challenge associated with front end development is that the tools and techniques used to create the front end of a website change constantly, and so the developer needs to constantly be aware of how the field is developing.

A front-end developer architects and develops websites and applications using web technologies, like HTML, CSS, and JavaScript, which run on the Open Web Platform or act as compilation input for non-web platform environments, like React Native. Have you ever heard about HTML, CSS, and JavaScript?

These technologies are actually the holy trinity in the front-end web development world. Also, the front-end developer can use different frameworks, like Angular, React, Vue.js and others, so your searching criteria as a recruiter can be based on these technologies too.

In their day-to-day operations, front-end developers write code in their language, which is then compiled (or "translated") by a browser like Google. The result is, essentially, a website: the banners, fonts, embedded images, and other visual aspects you regularly come across when visiting sites on the internet. As such, their tasks are one of the most crucial aspects of the overall web development process. After all, without a cohesive, inviting visual appearance that invites visitors to stick around, almost every other effort is wasted.

Usual front-end development search terms you can use for your recruiting purposes can be: front-end developer, JavaScript developer, web designer, and HTML/CSS developer, React developer, Angular developer, etc.

Screening questions based on requirements:

Q: What are the basic skills that a front-end developer needs to have?
A: Front-end developers need to have knowledge in HTML/CSS, JavaScript, one or more JavaScript frameworks, and SEO tools for website content creation. Experience in WordPress is additional plus.

Q: How to ensure that your website is user-friendly?
A: Front-end developer needs to take care of UX (User Experience) to imagine and structure a web page that cultivates a user experience by optimizing it for mobile phones and other devices.

Q: When is a CSS float used?
A: Float is used when you want to push an element of your website to the right or left and cover it with other elements around it.

6. Full Stack Developer
Full-stack developers are experts in both the front-end and back-end fields, so it is a full stack of technologies that make up a website. They are proficient in both front-end and back-end

languages and frameworks, as well as in server, network and hosting environments. To get to this breadth and depth of knowledge, most full-stack developers will have spent at least 5+ years working in a variety of different professional roles and earned a bachelor's degree in IT, Computer Science, Engineering, or a related field. They also tend to be well-versed in both business logic and user experience, meaning they are not only well-equipped to get hands on but can also guide and consult on strategy too.

A full-stack web developer is a person who can develop both client and server software. In addition to mastering HTML and CSS, he or she should be able to demonstrate proficiency with:

- Browser programming (using JavaScript, jQuery, Angular, or Vue).
- Server programming (using PHP, C#, Python, or Node).
- Database programming (using SQL, SQLite, or MongoDB).
- Delivering services and applications leveraging containers (using Kubernetes and AWS EKS).
- Delivering serverless computing solutions (using Google Cloud Functions and AWS Lambdas).
- Continuous integration and deployment practices.
- Integrating applications leveraging REST and messaged-based integrations (using queuing

technologies such as RabbitMQ, Kafka, or Google Pub/Sub).
- Using cloud computing platforms (like Microsoft Azure, Amazon AWS, and Google Cloud Platform).
- Using a full stack of modern web technologies and frameworks (like React, Java, Spring, etc.).
- Using relational database languages and tools (like SQL, Hibernate, or Liquibase).

Some additional qualifications (yes, there's more!) for a full stack developer include:
- 3+ years of experience as a software developer using standard web technologies (HTML, CSS, etc.).
  AND/OR
- 3+ years of experience as a software developer using Java and JavaScript.

Usual full-stack search terms you can use for your recruiting purposes can be: full-stack developer, front-end and back-end developer, client and server-side developer, database developer, etc.

Screening questions based on requirements:

Q: What are the most important skills that a Full-Stack Developer must have?
A: Proficiency in front-end technologies (HTML/CSS, JavaScript and at least one JavaScript framework), back-end technologies (PHP, Python, C#, Node.js or

back-end framework), as well as databases handling code version control (Git, GitHub).

Q: What is Continuous Integration?
A: Continuous Integration is the process of using codes that are specially designed & automated for testing. Web developers use this process to integrate codes several times a day. These codes are checked automatically to detect and fix errors.

Q: Why use NoSQL databases?
A: These are used for large sets of distributed data. These are very efficient in analyzing large size unstructured data that may be stored at multiple virtual servers of the cloud.

7. Quality Engineer (Quality Assurance)

A Quality Engineer works within the quality assurance (QA) team to ensure the overall quality of a manufactured product and is tasked with creating documentation, devising quality tests, and defining the criteria a test result should meet. They play a key role in fixing issues when they arise.

Quality engineers work closely with manufacturing suppliers to ensure turbine parts and components are produced according to product specifications. When a problem or working error is reported, they analyze the root cause of the issue, develop and implement a plan to improve performance, and monitor and evaluate improvements. Quality engineers keep detailed records of product and equipment inspections, root cause analyses, corrective action plans, and other reporting requirements.

It's also important to know the difference between testing and QA. Though they might seem similar, there is a key factor that slightly separates the two:

Testing vs. QA
- Testing focuses on specific activities to discover bugs and issues within the product before customers do.
  Whereas...
- QA focuses on the overall process of product development to ensure it remains efficient under various conditions.

This might sound a bit confusing at first, especially since the main purpose of either is to make a great product. The more you look into the two, however, you'll begin to see where they split: It should help to think of testing as an "activity," while QA is a "process."

That doesn't mean that testing isn't included in the QA lifecycle, however. In fact, it makes up the bulk of a quality engineer's tasks (which is to say, there's quite a few to cover). Let's review some of the main areas a QA candidate might need to know.

Manual vs. Automated Testing

- Manual testing is performed by a human tester.
- Automated testing is performed by automation tools designed to execute specific test cases.

Testing Types
- Functional
  - Unit testing
  - Integration testing
  - System testing
  - Smoke testing
  - Regression testing
  - Acceptance testing
- Non-functional
  - Performance testing
  - Load testing
  - Stress testing
  - Security testing
  - Compatibility testing
  - Usability testing
  - Localization testing
  - Compliance testing

Testing Tools
- Java
  - Junit
- Cross-platform
  - Selenium
- JavaScript
  - Jest
  - Mocha

- C#
  - NUnit
  - XUnit
- PHP
  - PHPUnit

Fortunately, it's unlikely that a single quality engineer would ever be tasked with overseeing so many different responsibilities. Most operations delegate these tasks according to specific QA roles, allowing engineers to refine their craft in one area.

QA Roles
- Manual tester
- Software tester
- QA engineer
- QA manager
- Test automation engineer
- Automation tester
- Senior Software QA Engineer
- Quality Assurance Engineer

To be successful in any of these roles, a quality engineer will usually need to possess the following skills:
1. Attention to details: Quality engineers must have attention to detail to ensure that products are being manufactured, installed, or are operating to the required specifications.
2. Analysis
3. Critical thinking

4. Problem-solving skills

Usual Quality Engineer search terms you can use for your recruiting purposes can be: QA Engineer, QC Engineer, Quality Specialist, Quality Engineer, etc.

Screening questions based on requirements:

Q: What is a Project Quality Plan?
A: The Project Quality Plan is one of the most important documents. It is essentially the guidelines of the project as it establishes a number of deliverable materials and standard work procedures.

Q: What checks and balances do you use to ensure that you don't make mistakes?
A: There can be used different testing systems and tools for measuring the quality and detecting errors. Also, taking notes or using a digital system can assess tasks or project steps.

8. DevOps Engineer
DevOps is the combination of cultural philosophies, practices, and tools that increases an ability to deliver software at high velocity: evolving and improving products at a faster pace than organizations using traditional software development and infrastructure management processes. DevOps engineers use practices to automate processes that certainly have been manual and slow. They use a technology stack and

tooling, which help them operate and evolve applications quickly and reliably. These tools also help engineers independently accomplish tasks that normally would have required help from other teams, and this further increases a team's velocity. It's important to mention that DevOps engineers are team players, and collaboration with other team members is crucial.

DevOps engineers often write code in Linux operating systems, Python, on AWS, or something similar, so having such a skillset is a big plus through the recruiting process.

Usual DevOps engineering search terms you can use for your recruiting purposes can be: DevOps engineer, Cloud engineer, AWS engineer, Azure, and Docker.

Screening questions based on requirements:

Q: What are the must-have skills every DevOps engineer needs to have?
A: DevOps engineers need to have strong knowledge in cloud computing and database technologies (SQL, MySQL), as well as experience in running virtual machines, maintenance, and scaling code. Experience in the Linux operating system is a big plus.

Q: What is the difference between DevOps and agile methodology?

A: DevOps is a culture that allows the development and the operations team to work together, including continuous development, testing, integration, deployment, and monitoring the software lifecycle. Agile is a software development methodology that focuses on iterative, incremental, small, and rapid releases of software, along with customer feedback, including locating errors and fixing them together with the customer.

Q: Which are the best DevOps tools?
A: The most popular ones are: Selenium. Git, Jenkins, Ansible, and Docker.

9. Data Scientist

Data scientists are analytical experts who utilize their skills in both technology and social science to find trends and manage data. They use industry knowledge and contextual understanding to uncover solutions to business challenges. Data scientists are big data wranglers, gathering and analyzing large sets of structured and unstructured data. A data scientist's role combines computer science, statistics, and mathematics. They analyze, process, and model data then interpret the results to create actionable plans for companies and other organizations.

There are various skills that every Data Scientist need to master:

1. Statistics and Algorithms

2. R and Python programming language
3. Data Wrangling and Exploration
4. Machine Learning
5. Deep Learning
6. Big Data Processing
7. Data Visualization
8. Data Mining and Warehousing
9. MongoDB, Oracle, Microsoft Azure, Cloudera, and other big data platforms.

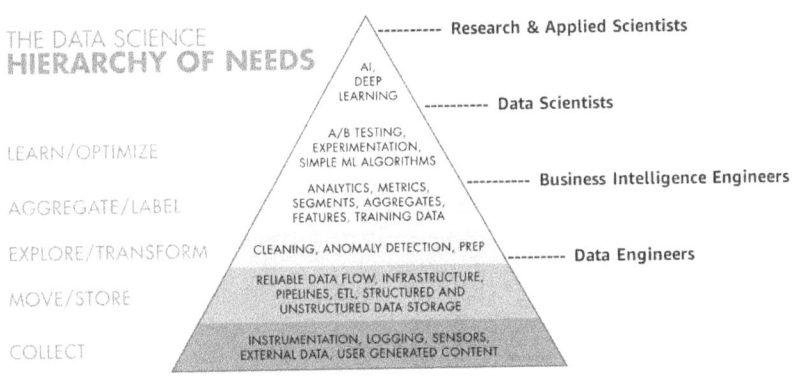

With this extensive knowledge at their side, tech companies trust data scientists to be able to complete a variety of essential tasks, such as:

- Gathering structured and unstructured data (i.e., data that wasn't stored in a database) through surveys, webs scraping, and Application Programming Interfaces (APIs).
- Performing undirected and direct research to help the organization solve problems.

- "Clean" collected data to eliminate irrelevant information.
- Identify new algorithms and establish new automated programs to help streamline repetitive work.
- Discover improvements that will increase ROI and make existing procedures and/or strategies more effective.

Usual data scientist search terms you can use for your recruiting purposes can be: Data Analyst, Data Engineer, Database Administrator, Machine Learning Engineer, Data Scientist, and Business Analyst.

Screening questions based on requirements:

Q: Which are the basic qualities every Data Scientist needs to have?
A: Communication skills, teamwork, leadership, working enthusiasm, strong morals, and discipline.

Q: Why is Big Data important?
A: Big data is changing how even the smallest companies do business as data collection and interpretation become more accessible. New, innovative, and cost-effective technologies are constantly emerging and improving, which makes it incredibly easy for any organization to seamlessly implement big data solutions.

10. Security Engineer

Security engineering focuses on designing computer systems that can deal with disruptions such as natural disasters or malicious cyber-attacks.

Security engineers develop and supervise data and technology security systems to help prevent breaches, taps, and leaks connected with cybercrime. Alternate titles for this career while recruiting include: information assurance engineer, information systems security engineer, and information security engineer.

There are nine total areas within the cyber security field that security engineers can investigate, each with their own technical focuses.

1. **Data Protection**
   - Data encryption
   - Data loss prevention
   - Database security
   - Blockchain
   - Data access governance

2. **Identity Management**
   - Data access
   - Identity & access management

3. **Application Security**
   - Web application security
   - Component's security

4. **Cloud Application Security**

- Containers
- Compliance
- Cloud Workspace

5. **Network Security**

6. **Foundational Security**
   - Network Security
     - Firewall, SSL, DDoS Mitigation, Remote Access
   - Data Center Security
     - Platform, Storage Network
   - Endpoint Security
     - Wireless devices connected to corporate networks

7. **Security Operations**
   - Monitoring & Operations
   - Vulnerability Assessment & Management
   - Change Management
   - Threat Detection & Analysis
   - Orchestration & Automation
   - Incident Management & Response

8. **Risk & Compliance**
   - GDPR
   - PCI DSS

9. **IoT Security**

In accordance with the wide range of focus areas available, there are nearly just as many roles a cybersecurity expert can take on.

Entry Level
- Cyber Intern
- Information Security Intern
- Network and Security Intern
- Cyber Security Apprentice
- Pentester Trainee
- Junior Cyber Security Associate

Individual Contributors
- Cyber Security Analyst
- Security Engineer
- Data Security Analyst
- White Hat Hacker
- AWS Cloud Architect
- Cyber Security Risk Analyst
- Cyber Security Strategist
- Information Technology Specialist (Security)

Managers
- Cyber Security Manager
- Security Operations Center Manager
- Cyber Security Product Manager

Directors & VPs
- Cyber Security Lead
- Security Program Lead
- Cyber Security Product Lead
- VP Cyber Security

- Cyber Security Director
- Cyber Security Executive

C-level
- Chief Security Officer
- Head of Cyber Security
- Head of Cyber Defense

Security engineers need many technical skills. Some of the skills security engineers need to master are IT support skills, familiarity with Unix/Windows, understanding of how to monitor security systems, and knowledge of securities systems infrastructure. Penetration testing and computer network security are always welcome in the cyber-security industry.

Screening questions based on requirements:

Q: How can information security be achieved?
A: Knowing what needs to be protected, developing clear models of cloud systems, and leveraging threat intelligence can be crucial steps in achieving the highest level of information security.

Q: What tools and techniques should a security engineer be familiar with?
A: There is a spectrum of tools available to security engineers. These include frameworks, libraries, and other tools used to track, defend against, and determine the probable causes of security breaches. The tools are often used for detecting

social engineering, viruses, spyware, phishing, or fake site overflows.

Q: What is a security control?
A: Security controls are parameters implemented to protect various forms of data and infrastructure important to an organization. Any type of safeguard used to avoid, detect, or minimize security risks is considered a security control.

11. Data Analyst

A data analyst collects processes and performs statistical analyses on a large dataset. They discover how data can be used to answer questions and solve problems. With the development of computers and an ever-increasing move toward technological intertwinement, data analysis has evolved.

There are a few key responsibilities that every data analyst needs to have:

1. Designing and maintaining data systems and databases
2. Mining data from primary and secondary sources
3. Using statistical tools to interpret data sets
4. Preparing reports for executive leadership
5. Collaborating with programmers, engineers, and organizational leaders
6. Creating appropriate documentation that allows stakeholders to understand the steps of the data analysis

Here's essential skills that every data analyst needs to master, very similar to data scientists:

1. SQL or Structured Query Language (this programming language is possibly the most important skill for data analysts to have)
2. Microsoft Excel for data representation and collecting
3. Critical Thinking
4. R or Python Programming
5. Data visualization
6. Presentation skills
7. Machine learning

Usual data analyst search terms you can use for your recruiting purposes can be: data analyst, data engineer, database administrator, or data statistician.

Screening questions based on requirements:

Q: What does Data Cleansing mean?
A: Data cleansing primarily refers to the process of detecting and removing errors and inconsistencies from the data to improve data quality.

The best ways to clean data are:
- Segregating data, according to their respective attributes
- Breaking large chunks of data into small datasets and then cleaning them
- Analyzing the statistics of each data column

Q: Which are the best tools used for data analysis?
A: The most popular ones are:

- Tableau
- Google Fusion Tables
- Google Search Operators
- KNIME
- RapidMiner
- Solver
- OpenRefine
- NodeXL

Q: What is the difference between data profiling and data mining?
A: Data profiling focuses on analyzing individual attributes of data, thereby providing valuable information on data attributes such as data type, frequency, length, along with their discrete values and value ranges. On the other hand, data mining aims to identify unusual records, analyze data clusters, and sequence discovery, to name a few.

12. Solution Architect

Solution architecture is a practice of designing, describing, and managing the solution engineering in relation to specific business problems. A solution architect is the person in charge of leading the practice and introducing the overall technical vision for a solution.

Solution architecture is one of the foundational elements of any project or organization. It is the instrumental backbone that holds things together. In a way, the solution architect's job is to build a bridge between enterprise and technical architecture. In other words, provide the infrastructure that will make the system efficient.

Solution Architect's must-have skills and qualifications:

- 8+ years of technical background and experience in development
- Ability to consult management and engineering teams with technical advice
- Communication skills
- Deep analytical skills and the ability to see the connections between layers of business operations

Using these skills, a solution architect can expect to follow some of the following tasks in day-to-day operations.

- Making sure new systems will fit the enterprise's existing "environment", including application architectures, operating systems, operational processes, and more.
- Identifying and accounting for project constraints like time, resources, scope, tech, risks, and cost.
- Translating details from tech projects into digestible language that non-tech employees (like recruiters!) can understand.

Usual solution architect search terms you can use for your recruiting purposes can be: solution architect, business analyst, or project management consultant.

Screening questions based on requirements:

Q: What are the strengths of any solutions architect?
A: Solutions architects are responsible not only for providing hardware and software selections and determining which choices have the best impact on a business outcome, but they also have a solid understanding of business and an ability to communicate effectively with internal teams and customers

Q: What is scalability?
A: Scalability is the ability of a system, network, or process to handle a growing amount of load by adding more resources. The addition of resources can be done in two ways
1. Scaling Up - This involves adding more resources to the existing nodes. For example, adding more RAM, storage, or processing power.
2. Scaling Out - This involves adding more nodes to support more users.

Q: What is lower latency interaction?
A: Low latency means that there is very little delay between the time you request something and the

time you get a response. It just means that data can be sent quicker because the connection has already been established, so no extra packet round trips are required to establish the TCP connection.

13. System Engineer

A computer system engineer develops, tests, and evaluates software and personal computers by combining their knowledge of engineering, computer science, and math analysis. Contrary to popular belief, computer systems engineers do not merely engineer computer technology.

A systems engineer is generally responsible for the hardware/Operating System platform as well as the commercial, open source and/or in-house services. Coding generally comes in the form of configuration management tools using a common language-inspired DSL. Preferred skills include:

1. Ability to know when you are done
2. An analytical brain
3. Knowledge of systems engineering software Tool(s)
4. Strong organizational skills

A few responsibilities system engineers are commonly tasked with are:
- Monitoring and managing installed infrastructure and systems
- Helping to design operational support systems

- Writing new scripts that reduce the need for human intervention on tasks
- Working alongside other IT teams and vendors to solve issues
- Remaining in contact with the Project Manager to communicate updates about system development

Search Terms include:

- Linux, Unix or Windows Systems Administration: Redhat, Solaris, SUSE, Ubuntu, etc.
- LDAP Configuration
- Usually have an understanding of Networking and routing protocols
- Automation or Scripting experience, usually in bash or shell (PowerShell for Windows) but could also have other OOP experience
- Root cause troubleshooting and diagnosis experience

Usual system engineer search terms you can use for your recruiting purposes can be: system engineer, computer architect, or system analyst, etc.

Screening questions based on requirements:

Q: What qualities should a Systems Engineer possess?

A: Experience in the field of systems engineering, patience and perseverance in working with complicated systems, as well as analytical skills for growing the business.

Q: Describe the process of building a software or system.
A: The process comprises of four steps:
- Analyzing the requirements, including the suitability of the environment
- System analysis control to measure and manage risks
- Allocation/functional analysis to allocate performance and other requirements
- Synthesis of a suitable design to configure various system elements and items

14. Systems Administrator

Network and computer systems administrators are responsible for the day-to-day operation of these networks. They organize, install, and support an organization's computer systems, including local area networks (LANs), wide area networks (WANs), network segments, intranets, and other data communication systems.

The must-have skills for system administrators are:
- Problem-Solving and Administration
- Networking
- Cloud
- Security and Monitoring
- IoT and Mobile Device Management

- Scripting Programming Languages
- Knowledge of networks
- Communication

The main responsibilities a system administrator oversees include:
- Administrative tasks like resource monitoring, investigating event log errors and warnings, managing security permissions, and more.
- Performing routine audits of existing and backup systems.
- Maintain internal infrastructure, including desktop and laptops, routers, firewalls, servers, security updates, printers, LANs, WANs, and intranets.
- Working alongside the help desk and other IT personnel to solve issues.

Usual system administrator searches you can use for your recruiting purposes can be: system administrator, system engineer, computer architect, system analyst, or network administrator.

Screening questions based on requirements:

Q: What is the difference between a system and a network administrator?
A: The difference between these two roles is that a network administrator oversees the network (a group of computers connected together) while a system administrator oversees the computer

systems and all the parts that make a computer function.

Q: What is the role of Windows Server?
A: Windows Server is an operating system that uses a centralized computer that provides specific functions and predetermined rules for users and computers connected to a network.

Q: What is an active directory?
A: Active Directory is used for user and computer authentication within a domain. It can also enforce security policies and install software to computers connected to a domain.

15. Applications Engineer

Application engineers, sometimes called software application developers, create, design, and test computer software programs. Their job may require them to create specific applications to meet clients' needs, modify existing applications to fix problems, or install new applications.

Systems applications engineers provide front-end support to users, making sure that the product is usable for them and is easy to navigate. The primary work of an individual in this position is to develop and implement software and engineering modules for testing and measurement of automation systems.

Preferable skills that every application engineer needs:
- Developing and improving software applications
- Familiarity with hardware
- Superior troubleshooting skills

Usual applications engineer search terms you can use for your recruiting purposes can be: application engineer, software application developer, system application developer, system application engineer.

Screening questions based on requirements:

Q: Which are the main qualities that every application engineer needs to have?
A:
- Strong knowledge of software and all the coding skills
- Project managing abilities and strong quantitative skills
- Higher-level calls that will ensure software quality

Q: Which programming languages are required for application engineers?
A: There are plenty of them, like C#, Java, SQL, PHP, & C++.

Q: Explain the IP/TCP protocol.
A: This is the process that is used in an IP and TCP network to build connections between the client

and server. It is a process that has three steps that need both the server and the client to exchange the synchronization and knowledge of packets prior to the real data communication process beginning.

16. Data Engineer

Data engineers are responsible for finding trends in data sets and developing algorithms to help make raw data more useful to the enterprise. Data engineers are often responsible for building algorithms to help give easier access to raw data, but to do this, they need to understand the company's or client's objectives.

Essential data engineer skills are:
- Database systems (SQL and NoSQL)
- Data warehousing solutions
- Machine learning
- Python, Java, Scala and R programming languages
- Knowledge of algorithms and data structures

Educational Background:
- Bachelors or Masters in Engineering, Computer Science, or a related quantative field

Common Job Titles:
- Data Engineer
- Big Data Developer/Engineer
- Hadoop Developer/Engineer

Required Skillsets:

- Proficiency in writing complex, highly-optimized **SQL** queries across large data sets
- Proficiency in **Python** or **other scripting language** such as **Scala, Perl, KornShell**
- Experience with **data modeling, data warehousing,** and **building ETL pipelines**
- Experience with **Big Data Technologies** (*Hadoop, Hive, Hbase, Pig, Spark, etc.*)
- Experience with **data warehouse/database products** (*Redshift, Oracle, NoSQL etc.*)
- In-depth understanding of **database performance and optimization techniques** (*partitioning, distribution, and indexing*)
- Experience **analyzing** and **interpreting** data

Usual data engineer search terms you can use for your recruiting purposes can be: data engineer, data analyst, data scientist, or statistician.

Screening questions based on requirements:

Q: What is Data Engineering?
A: Data engineering is a term used in big data. It focuses on the application of data collection and research. The data generated from various sources are just raw data. Data engineering helps to convert this raw data into useful information.

Q: What is Data Modeling?
A: Data modeling is the method of documenting complex software design as a diagram, so that anyone can easily understand. It is a conceptual

representation of data objects that are associated between various data objects and the rules.

Q: How can you best deploy a big data solution?
A: There are 3 steps to do it:
1. Integrate data using data sources like RDBMS, SAP, MySQL, and Salesforce.
2. Store data extracted data in either NoSQL database or HDFS.
3. Deploy big data solutions using processing frameworks like Pig, Spark, and MapReduce.

17. IT Manager

Computer and information systems managers, or information technology managers, are the guides who help organizations navigate the always-changing labyrinth that is modern technology. These all-important employees deliver short- and long-term visions for the company's technology needs and goals.

In addition to some level of technical experience, IT managers are required to have at least a bachelor's degree education in IT, preferably with well-rounded major such as computer science, information technology, or management information systems.

Skills needed to be an IT Manager:
- Strong technical skills
- Negotiation skills
- Strong financial and organizational skills

- Conflict management
- Strong project management skills
- Presentation and writing skills

Usual IT Manager search terms you can use for your recruiting purposes can be: IT manager, IT project manager, software architect, etc.

Screening questions based on requirements:

Q: What is the importance of an IT policy?
A: It's the role of the IT manager to create new policies when IT standards, regulations, or laws are changed. The policies show workers how to use information systems and IT-related business services according to the changes.

Q: How do you gather system and user requirements?
A:
- Take good notes
- Go over creative requirements
- Make annotations
- Write the requirements document

18. Mobile Developer – Android and iOS
Mobile application development is the process of creating software applications that run on a mobile device, and a typical mobile application utilizes a network connection to work with remote computing resources. Hence, the mobile development process involves creating installable

software bundles (code, binaries, assets, etc.) and implementing back-end services such as data access with testing the application on target devices.

There are 2 popular types of mobile app development, one for Android and one for iOS operating systems. The native development programming language for Android OS applications is Java, so the most popular languages used for building Android applications are Java, Kotlin, C and C++ (depending on the project type). For iPhones, the best programming language for building iOS mobile apps is Swift and Objective-C. However, applications specifically developed to be cross-platform are best suited for C# and JavaScript languages. Here's a breakdown:

Mobile App Developers
- Native apps
  - iOS app development
    - Objective-C
    - Swift
  - Android app development
    - Java
    - Kotlin
- Cross-platform apps
  - JavaScript
    - React Native
    - Ionic
    - Titanium Appcelerator
  - C#

- Xamarin
  o Dark
    - Flutter

Usual mobile developer search terms you can use for your recruiting purposes can be: mobile app developer, mobile app engineer, Android developer, iOS developer, etc.

Screening questions based on requirements:

Q: What are cards in mobile development?
A: Cards are quickly becoming one of the best design patterns for mobile devices. They collect individual pieces of content aggregated together into one experience.

Q: When should you use a Fragment, rather than an Activity?
A: The code used to create an Activity is fundamentally more involved than the code used to create a Fragment. The developer should acknowledge that the best practice is to only use Activities when you need to swap the entire screen and use fragments everywhere else.

Q: What is managed object context in iOS?
A: A managed object context is basically a temporary "scratch pad" in an application for a related collection of objects. These objects collectively represent an internally consistent view of one or more persistent stores. A single managed

object instance exists in one and only one context, but multiple copies of an object can exist in different contexts.

19. Sales Engineer

A sales engineer is someone who sells complex scientific and technological products or services to businesses. They must have extensive knowledge of the products' parts and functions and must understand the scientific processes that make these products work.

Key responsibilities that sales engineers have are:
- Supporting sales executives with solutions selling into a prospective account base
- Partnering with sales executives to plan, prepare and execute strategic deals in complex sales cycles
- Modeling the financial business case associated with each sales opportunity

Some sales engineers have large territories and travel extensively. Because sales regions may cover several states, sales engineers may be away from home for several days or even weeks at a time. Other sales engineers cover a smaller region and spend only a few nights away from home. So, some of their crucial skills are:

- A solid technical background
- Good business sense
- Teamwork

- The ability to build relationships with clients quickly
- Analytical and problem-solving skills
- Fluently speaking foreign languages

Usual sales engineer search terms you can use for your recruiting purposes can be: sales engineer, sales executive, solution engineer, customer engineer, pre-sales engineer, etc.

Screening questions based on requirements:

Q: How does a sales engineer deal with conflict resolution?
A: Taking action from various angles instead of forcing a solution is the best practice. Forcing a solution may put a bandage on the issue for a moment. But taking time to consider options and perspectives can be the difference between a hardworking sales team and a sales team that is distracted by discomfort.

Q: What is the best approach to a typical sales call with a new or returning client?
A: It's always good to focus on finding out the client's needs and wants right off the bat. Using leading questions to help them flesh out the idea in their mind is a good idea too. This applies to both regular sales calls and sales calls about unexpected problems or tech support.

Q: Describe the sales process cycle.

A: Prospecting, approach, need assessment, presentation, meeting objections, gaining commitment, and follow-up.

20. UX Designer

UX design is the process of designing (digital or physical) products that are useful, easy to use, and delightful to interact with. It's about enhancing the experience that people have while interacting with your product and making sure they find value in what you're providing.

A UX designer is concerned with the entire process of acquiring and integrating a product, including aspects of branding, design, usability, and function. It is a story that begins before the device is even in the user's hands.

A UX designer is an advocate for the end-users of a website or product. Key areas of focus include information architecture, user research, branding, visual design, and content. They need to empathize with their subjects, tell a story well, and possess strong creative, technical, and problem-solving skills.

UX designer must have the following skills:
- High researching skills
- Collaborative skills
- Wire-framing and UI prototyping
- Visual communication
- Interaction design

- Information architecture (IA)
- Analytical skills
- User empathy

Also, UX designers use many programming languages, especially back-end ones, like Python or Ruby. Generally, UX designers don't use code, but it is important to understand any JavaScript prototype too.

Usual search terms you can use for UX designers for your recruiting purposes can be: UX designer, UX/UI designer, User Experience designer, or UX engineer.

Screening questions based on requirements:

Q: What is the basic process of UX Designing?
A: Research, design, usability testing, serving.

Q: How do UX designers decide which features to add to the product?
A: In the context of building a new piece of software, the MVP (minimum viable product) method could be developed to make a clear decision. In the context of an existing product, the focus should be on the fundamentals of product strategy.

Q: What can be done to locate the problem when an UX project goes wrong?
A: Elaborating on these questions can locate the problem and show the solution:
   1. What went wrong?

2. Why did it go wrong?
3. What can be done to address the failure?
4. What was learned from that experience?
5. What to do to resolve the addressed failure?

21 .Net Developer

.NET Software Developer is a software developer who specializes in building software for Microsoft's Windows platform. They work with programming languages compatible with Microsoft .NET framework, including VB.NET, C# and F#.

.NET developer, in particular, needs some more skills:

- Proficiency with C# is a must, with a familiarity of its coding environment
- Knowledge of the .NET technologies
- Strong understanding of the structure and logic of Object-Oriented programming

Usual search terms you can use for .NET Developer for your recruiting purposes can be: .NET developer, .NET web developer, or .NET architect.

Screening questions based on requirements:

Q: What is the .NET Framework?
A: .NET is a Microsoft framework designed to help developers work with different coding languages. In simple terms, it's a virtual machine that assists with the compilation, conversion, and execution of code within a development framework. Using .NET,

developers can create form- and web-based applications and services.

Q: What languages .NET Framework support?
A: The most common languages are VB.NET, COBOL, Perl, C#, C++, and F# languages.

Q: What is the difference between managed and unmanaged code?
A: Managed code is managed by and runs inside the CLR and needs the .NET Framework to execute. Unmanaged code, on the other hand, does not need the CLR to execute. Unmanaged code is formulated from a language independent of the .NET Framework and, therefore, uses its independent environment for execution and compiling.

22. EDI Engineer

An electronic data interchange (EDI) engineer facilitates the exchange of electronic data within a company or between two entities by creating a computer system. This position in the field of information technology is ideal for those who love to solve problems and work with computers.

An EDI developer is an EDI software specialist mainly using SQL programming language. SQL is a type of database that processes corporate transactions (such as electronic data interchange). You can generate reports of SQL database activity.

EDI developers are also in charge of developing, testing, and implementing EDI transaction maps.

Tasks and responsibilities expected from every EDI engineer:

- Designing and developing a system for the exchange of information
- Implementing EDI solutions
- Setting up systems for new trading partners
- Updating and improving interactions with existing trading partners
- Using EDI mapping tools and cross-reference tables

Usual search terms you can use for EDI Engineer for your recruiting purposes can be: EDI engineer, EDI specialist, or EDI analyst.

Screening questions based on requirements:

Q: Who typically uses EDI?
A: EDI is used in nearly all the major industries such as automotive, aerospace, retail, finance, and CPG sectors. EDI is regarded as the standard for the electronic exchange of documents from one company to another.

Q: How is EDI Used?
A: EDI is used as a strategic tool to reduce expenses, streamline business procedures, and create a competitive advantage.

Q: What is an EDI business partner?
A: An EDI business partner is simply another company that you exchange documents with. Most OEMs will have a large network of business partners which are sometimes referred to as 'Trading Communities'.

23. Support Engineer

Support engineers serve as experts in the products that their company manufactures and develops. They find solutions to problems with the products and help customers work through technical difficulties. Job duties may include: debugging, scripting, test, analyzing code, and application support. As such, candidates should be able to demonstrate proficiency in specific technologies like Windows and Cisco, as well as proven experience in troubleshooting software & hardware issues.

The support engineer is responsible for offering application and technical support to the users. They have to respond and resolve the support requests and service tickets. It is a part of their job to identify, diagnose, and rectify any issues in computer hardware, software, services, and applications.

Areas that a support engineer may operate in include:
- Application support

- - Application support
  - Help Desk Analyst
- Technical support
  - Technical Support
  - Desktop Support
  - Helpdesk Engineer
- Hardware support
- Network support
- Accounts support

The key requirements that each support engineer needs to know are: Providing excellent customer service for clients requesting software installation, updates/upgrades on their server. Also, they can be described as motivated self-starters and self-learners possessing strong customer service, listening, e-mail communication, technical problem-solving skills.

Usual search terms you can use for support engineer for your recruiting purposes can be:
- Technical support specialist
- IT support specialist
- IT support analyst
- IT support engineer
- IT support manager
- Application Support Engineer
- Helpdesk Specialist
- Customer Support Specialist
- Cloud Support Engineer
- IT specialist (Customer Support)
- Help Desk operator

This role requires the following disciplines:

- The ability to solve problems at their root, by stepping back to understand the broader context.
- A strong aptitude for troubleshooting and problem-solving.
- The ability to maintain SLA's through the implementation of proactive issue detection and reporting.
- The ability to set up, configure and monitor systems to prevent prolonged outages.
- A basic understanding of operating system administration.
- The ability to write and review accurate and complete support procedures, system documentation, and issue tracking entries.
- Good judgment and instincts in decision-making.
- The ability to prioritize in a complex, fast-paced environment.

Screening questions based on requirements:

Q: How can you go about diagnosing problems with a client's computer systems?
A: A strong knowledge of troubleshooting methodology and company best practices is required to detect the client's problem and solve it immediately. Many tools and strategies are used depending on the client's problem type.

Q: Describe the difference between SDK and an API.
A: SDK is a kit that offers tools, code samples, libraries, processes, guides, or relevant documents for creating software applications on specific platforms. On the other hand, API is an interface that allows the software to interact with each other.

Q: What is Ghost Imaging?
A: Ghost imaging (cloning) is a backup process driven by some software. It copies the hard disk contents to another server in one compressed file or a set of files which is referred to as an image. When needed, it can also change a ghost image back to its original form. It is often used during the reinstallation of OS.

General:
Q: What is a CDN?
A: A content delivery network is commonly used to serve static (images, JavaScript, CSS) assets quickly by caching regionally.

Q: Name some ways of debugging a client-side application.
A: Logging, debugger, breakpoints, Chrome Dev Tools, Firefox Developer Tools.

Q: What data structure is used to represent the DOM of a web page?
A: The document object model is a tree.

Q: What's the difference between asynchronous and synchronous code in the browser?
A: Asynchronous code is not waited on by the program and yields a result later in the life of a program. Examples: XML Http Request, HTTP requests, AJAX, fetch, set Timeout, and set Interval. Synchronous code is waited on by the program and yields a result before running the rest of the program.

CSS:
Q: Explain different approaches for positioning elements on a web page.
A: Using the CSS property "display" with values, such as block, inline-block, flex;
CSS Grid positioning; positioning elements absolutely or relatively; using floats.

Q: What is CSS selector specificity?
A: The count, depth, and weight of CSS selectors contribute to the selector's specificity. For example, an ID has a larger weight compared to a class and,

therefore, a greater specificity. When selectors are combined, the weight is additive. For example, a CSS selector that includes an ID and a class increases in specificity based on the weight of both the ID and class.

Q: What CSS feature can be used to create mobile responsive websites?
A: Media queries, @media, that target the width and height of a screen.

JavaScript:
Q: How is an arrow function different from a function?
A: An arrow function binds "this" to the function automatically.

Q: What's the difference between a Set and a Map?
A: A Set is a unique list of elements. A Map is a key-value store.

Q: What are the steps a browser takes to run JavaScript?
A: Load, parse, compile, evaluate.

Services:
Q: How many services, internal or external, does your product connect to and use?
A: Someone working in middle-tier should have a rough idea of the different services their website connects to.

Q: What are some use cases for service/server/webapp logs?
A: Access info, debugging, business analytics and metrics, operation analytics and metrics.

Q: Name some of your services' TPS (transactions-per-second). Rough estimates are acceptable.
A: Someone working in a middle-tier should have a rough idea of their system's scale.

24 Desktop App Developer

Desktop app developers are primarily responsible for programming, testing, and maintaining apps built for computers. The code the write is specifically created to run natively on operating systems like Windows, macOS, and Linux — *without* needing to be connected to the internet. (Essentially, these are like the "stock" apps that come right out of the box with your new laptop).

Like many IT roles, even desktop app developers can focus on certain niches within the field, as some platforms may require specific coding languages.

For instance, a cross-platform desktop app developer should know:

- Java language in the Swing framework
- JavaScript language in the Electron framework
- C++ language in the Qt framework
- Python language in the pyQt framework
- C# language in the Unity framework

Meanwhile, a platform-specific developer should have proficiency in one of the following landscapes:
- Windows
  - C# language in the WPF framework, WinForms, or UWP
- macOS
  - Objective-C language in the Cocoa framework
  - Swift language in the Cocoa framework

In day-to-day operations, a desktop app developer will be tasked with testing and debugging source code, analyzing existing applications for potential updates or fixes, creating new source code for new applications, and more. As such, a good candidate will need to possess good analytical skills, communication abilities, attention to detail, and technical prowess.

25. Hardware Engineer

A hardware engineer is a professional who designs, develops, and tests electronic components and systems, such as computer hardware, microprocessors, memory chips, and other devices. They work on the physical aspects of a computer or electronic system, rather than its software or programming.

Hardware engineers typically have a strong background in electrical engineering, computer engineering, or a related field, and are skilled in designing and implementing digital circuits, microcontrollers, and other electronic components. They work closely with software engineers to ensure that the hardware components of a system are properly integrated with the software.

Hardware engineers may work for a variety of companies, including computer hardware manufacturers, telecommunications firms, consumer electronics companies, and aerospace and defense contractors. They may be involved in all stages of the product development process, from initial design and prototyping to testing, manufacturing, and quality control.

Types of Hardware Engineers:

Innovation Design Engineer
An Innovation Design Engineer is a professional who uses their skills in engineering, design thinking, and innovation to create new products, services, or systems that address user needs and solve complex problems. They combine their technical expertise with creative thinking and user-centered design principles to come up with innovative solutions.

- Experience with Design for Operations and process design based on Lean Principles
- Fundamentals in Industrial Engineering including Lean/Toyota Production Systems

(TPS), value stream engineering, statistical process control (SPC), business case analysis, and ergonomic and safety assessment
- Experience working with Architects, General Contractors, and Engineers on greenfield and brownfield construction projects to integrate life safety, regulatory, structural, mechanical, electrical, plumbing, and low voltage requirements into the full project life cycle
- Bachelor's degree in engineering, operations, or a related field required

Mechanical Engineer

A mechanical engineer is a professional who applies principles of physics, mathematics, and materials science to design, analyze, manufacture, and maintain mechanical systems. These systems can include anything from engines and machines to structures and devices.

Mechanical engineers typically work on a variety of projects, including design, testing, and maintenance of mechanical systems. They use computer-aided design (CAD) software and other tools to create detailed schematics and blueprints, and then oversee the fabrication, installation, and operation of these systems. They may also be involved in troubleshooting and maintenance of mechanical systems to ensure that they operate efficiently and reliably.

- SolidWorks or similar CAD experience with best practices for part design, advanced assemblies, complex configuration management
- 3D modeling/drawings: Solidworks, ProE/CREO, AutoCAD
- FEA tools: Ansys, Solidworks and ProE/CREO both have Analysis tools built in as well
- Hands on experience crafting simple proof-of-concept models
- Thorough understanding and use of principals, theories and concepts in mechanical engineering
- Bachelor's Degree in Mechanical Engineering

Electrical Engineer

An electrical engineer is a professional who specializes in the design, development, and testing of electrical equipment, systems, and devices. They work with electricity and electromagnetism to create and improve a wide range of products and systems, from power generation and transmission to electronic devices and communication systems.

Electrical engineers typically have a strong background in mathematics and physics, and may specialize in one or more areas, such as power systems, control systems, signal processing, telecommunications, or electronics. They use specialized software and computer-aided design (CAD) tools to create schematics, designs, and models of electrical systems.

The work of an electrical engineer can involve a wide range of tasks, such as designing electrical circuits, testing and troubleshooting systems, and overseeing the installation and operation of electrical equipment. They may work in a variety of settings, including manufacturing plants, research and development labs, and engineering consulting firms.

- Methodologies/Tools used: OrCAD Capture, Cadence Allegro, Matlab and PSPICE, FPGAs, VHDL, microcontrollers, microprocessors, Lattice, Xilinx, Altera, IEC 60204, IEC 61508, ANSI RIA R15.06
- Basic Python and LabVIEW experience
- Linux based product OS testing and control.
- Experience in circuit level debug to the component level
- Electrical capture and layout tool experience with the desire for experience designing low-level interface boards for test fixtures
- BSEE or equivalent required

Manufacturing Engineer
A manufacturing engineer is a professional who is responsible for designing and improving manufacturing processes and systems. They use their expertise in engineering, materials science, and production techniques to design and implement efficient manufacturing processes that maximize productivity and minimize waste.

Manufacturing engineers typically work in manufacturing plants or factories, where they oversee the production of goods or components. They may be involved in all stages of the manufacturing process, from design and prototype development to production planning, quality control, and maintenance.

- Six Sigma, LEAN Manufacturing, DFM/DFT (Design for Manufacturing/Design for Test)
- Broad manufacturing commodity background (Mechanical and Electrical)
- commodity experience with one or more of the following: Metal Fabrication, Plastics (Primarily injection molding) and Printed Circuit Board Assemblies
- Industry standard tools for problem solving and risk management
- BSME/EE or equivalent

26. Business Intelligence Engineer

A Business Intelligence Engineer is a professional who designs, develops, and implements data solutions to help businesses make informed decisions. They use their expertise in data analytics, programming, and data warehousing to create systems that allow organizations to gather, store, and analyze large amounts of data.

Business Intelligence Engineers work with cross-functional teams, including data analysts, business analysts, and software developers, to understand business needs and develop solutions to meet those needs. They use tools such as SQL, Python, and Tableau to design and implement data models, develop data pipelines, and create reports and dashboards.

The role of a Business Intelligence Engineer is to create a unified view of data from different sources, to ensure data quality and consistency, and to develop scalable data solutions that can support business growth. They must be able to work with large and complex datasets, and have strong analytical skills to identify patterns and trends in the data.

Business Intelligence Engineers may work in a variety of industries, such as finance, healthcare, and retail, and may be employed by large corporations or startups. They play a critical role in helping organizations make data-driven decisions and gain a competitive advantage in their respective industries.

Educational Background:
- Bachelors or Masters degree in Engineering, Computer Sciences, or related field

Common Job Titles:
- Senior Data Analyst
- Business Intelligence Lead
- Business Intelligence Developer
- Business Intelligence Consultant

Required Skillsets:
- Experienced in data cleaning and wrangling using **SQL** and **Python**
- Experience with one or more industry standard analytics **visualization** tools such as Tableau, QuickSight and PowerBI
- Experience with **descriptive statistics** and **inferential statistics** *(e.g. hypothesis testing)*
- Strong **writing, presentation** and **communication** skills

Chapter 2: How to Search for Tech Candidates

Searching for tech candidates and finding the right talent for your business purposes is the most crucial step in the recruiting sector. There are different sites and places online where you can search for the right tech candidates and connect with your chosen one.

In this chapter, you will have a chance to learn how to expand your search outside of resumes to social networks, forums, and other community sites online. There are 28 sites explained here, so make yourself comfortable and stay tuned...

1. Stack Overflow

Stack Overflow is a kind of super technical version of Quora. Basically, it is a question-and-answer site for technical questions. Users can post questions, answer other users' questions, and vote for the answers on the site.
The types of people on this site are going to be programmers or those dealing with a programming language. If you need a programmer, this is likely where they are hanging out.
According to Social Talent, Stack Overflow is the third-best platform for finding programmers, so keep that in your mind while recruiting talents online.
There are two ways to search Stack Overflow for candidates that have the skills you are seeking. There is the "All User Search" free searching and the paid Stack Overflow careers site. Both are great options to locate the profiles of qualified developers.

If you want to use the "All User Search", this platform allows you to search profiles for profile information, in a roundabout way. The best way to search the platform is by using Google X-Ray. The main points of the profile you may want to include in your search string are location and the tags they have contributed to. The tags will give you information on the programming languages they are proficient in.

Examples of how to search on Stack Overflow:
- site:careers.stackoverflow.com "Java Developer"
- site:stackoverflow.com/users "Java Developer"

2. GitHub

GitHub is the world's largest open-sourced repository coding site online today. Currently, it has over 28 million users and over 57 million in repositories. With so many monthly active users sharing and learning about coding, it's a fantastic place for Talent Sourcers to find qualified talent specifically within the software development space.

There is a massive list of sourcing tools you can use to find and recruit users on GitHub. But here will be listed only a few of them as suggestions you can choose from:
1. **OctoHR** - This is one of the all-time favorite extensions for GitHub profiles recruiting. When viewing a profile, this tool will showcase the programming languages the user is currently using. You can then use this

in your recruiter emails when passively reaching out to a lead.

2. **GitHub Hovercard** - GitHub Hovercard provides neat Hovercards for GitHub. You can hover over any profile and get value information on any profile. It brings you instant access to user/repo/issue/commit information from anywhere on GitHub.

3. **GitHubber** - This tool dives into Github profiles and returns condensed and summarized information within your Github Search results.

4. **Coderstats** - A platform to tell you about user statistics on Github. You just need to enter the name / company name to see graphs about the technologies that the developer uses, the stars, the number of forked repositories.

Examples of how to search on GitHub:

- site:github.com software engineer ~resume
- site:github.com software developer ~cv
- site:github.com web developer

3. Angel.co

Angel.co is the largest startup community online and one of the best sites to do research for tech candidates. This platform has multiple options and purposes, like finding a job, registering as an investor and product exploring.

As a recruiter for tech candidates, there is an option for you to post a free job opportunity or to use angel.com free tools to build your team and manage a candidate pipeline, also for free. There are more than 2.5 million high-quality candidates, including 750,000 software engineers and developers, more than 170,000 designers, and more and more tech job seekers every day.

By clicking on the "Post a free job" button on the angel.com home page, a new tab will be opened where you can post a job for software engineers, developers, or any kind of programmers and wait for people to apply. You just need to sign up for a new account and post a job listing. Or you can do research on the platform and try to find job seekers for certain tech positions.
Examples of how to search on Angel.co:
- site:angel.co "software engineer"
- site:angellist.com "web developer"
- site:angel.co "Java developer"

4. HackerNews

HackerNews is a news aggregator forum site similar to Reddit, but it primarily focuses on start-ups, developers, and hacker-related news. Topics include anything that "good hackers" would find interesting. Its founder, Paul Graham, wanted to create a community that would recreate the way Reddit felt in the good old days when developers were still the main focus.

When opening up this site, you will find out that HackerNews has created a sub specifically for developers actively looking for new opportunities. This sub is a month-by-month page called: Ask HN: Who wants to be hired?

You will find thousands of developers who are actively looking for openings across the globe. These subpages will give you a wealth of information on an active candidate: contact information, resume, portfolio, LinkedIn, & GitHub or Stack Overflow profiles.

You can do research using Boolean strings within a Google:

- Ask HN: Who wants to be hired? "October 2020"
- Ask HN: Who wants to be hired? "February 2021"

Other examples of Boolean researching for recruiting:
- Ask HN: Who wants to be hired? (October 2019) | Hacker News
- Ask HN: Who wants to be hired? (November 2019) | Hacker News
- Ask HN: Who wants to be hired? (December 2020) | Hacker News
- Ask HN: Who wants to be hired? (January 2021) | Hacker News

5. Reddit

You may have heard of the popular online forum Reddit.com as a go-to place to get answers to your questions or find the latest news stories. One area you may not have associated with the fourth largest website online today is its potential for recruiting. Yes, you can use Reddit to source and recruit potential candidates online.

Technology gurus use this site daily to get news and research different topics. There are specific topics dedicated to the job search, and if you are not utilizing this for recruiting, you are missing out on some great advertising for your job.

To get started with using Reddit for recruiting, here are some tips and steps you should take to do it properly:

1. Start by checking out subreddits like r/forhire to see what is currently being posted for roles. Reddit is different from other platforms you may use for posting jobs, so you will want to make sure you are using it properly.

2. If you are looking for Programmers and Developers, they are very likely hanging out on Reddit. If your jobs are on this platform, you may get a more passive candidate that isn't actively checking out traditional job posting sites.

3. Decide which subreddit you are going to post your job to. Choose topics that are relevant to the job you are posting to attract the best candidate. Every subreddit has specific guidelines, so the first step is to carefully read these and follow them.

4. Reddit is all about getting your questions answered, so you need to do this for your job as well. People may ask questions directly in the subreddit or private message you. It's just good practice to be honest about the job anyway. Candidates should come into a job

knowing what to expect, so they can be successful.

Some tools you can use while recruiting on Reddit are:

- MetaReddit: Use this site to search all the subreddits and tags.
- RedditMetrics: Track what subreddits are trending on Reddit.
- Reddit Insights: Track users and other data using this site.

site:reddit.com/user "* * developer" "For Hire"

site:reddit.com/user ("* Engineer" OR "* Developer" OR "* Programmer") "remote work" ("about me" OR "personal website")

6. Slack

Slack is a spot where people get together to talk about common areas of interests. The interests are grouped by communities and channels where people can talk with other members with the same interests. Companies use it to communicate with teams quickly, and individuals use it to talk about many different topics. The site is also indexed, and every topic is saved and searchable.

You will be where your candidates hang out. Instead of hoping they check their LinkedIn account once every two months, you can be sure they will be actively engaged. You can converse with people who are interested in the topics you are recruiting for. The site is also quick with people answering very quickly to posts.

Slack is also searchable. If you are looking for a candidate with a specific skill set, you can search by that skillset to see what communities come up. You can then see who is active in the community and either post in the channel or send a direct message to those you are interested in. Slack even has a page on how you can use the app for recruiting. Their page is all about how you can use it to keep everyone in the loop on the recruiting process. If you are a recruiter in a small company, this could be a great way to keep everyone up to date real time. To use this app for recruiting purposes and getting in touch with the potential candidates, check out the different communities to see which would be the best for the talent you are targeting.

There is a list of Slack channels for communities by region you can use to search for a candidate from a specific country, like: USA (6 regions), Australia, U.K, New Zealand, Ireland, Argentina, Brazil, Germany, France, Poland, and India.

7. Software Guild

The Software Guild is an intensive, fast-paced program that teaches the skills required to be a software developer. Here you can find information about. NET/C# or Java and acquire the skills needed for entry-level positions.

As a recruiter, you need to know that this site is a kind of search engine for people who want to work as programmers, in short, searching for job seekers in the programming sector. You can type the keywords to find any resume, job or company.

Also, Software Guild is about contract programming. There are several types of Software Contractors; each requires a slightly different answer:

1. **Temporary Hire:** These are folks that really want a full-time, permanent job but will take a contract job as a temporary fill in. Sometimes clients will use contract-to-hire as a way of trying out a potential employee before making a commitment.
2. **Consultant:** This is the other end of the spectrum where these folks are specialists in some specific area and have already established themselves with a lot of contacts.
3. **Contract coding:** Most software contractors fall into this area. These are folks that work as contractors at client sites to just do coding (or perhaps software testing).

To do your recruiting activities, you just need to open up the Software Guild platform by typing scguild.com in your browser, and you can use it totally free for researching programming candidate resumes and similar data.

8. Medium - r/programming

Medium is a place to read articles on the Internet, as well as a blogging platform, like Wordpress or Blogger. Medium is the new project from the guys who brought you Twitter. It's chaotically produced by a combination of top-notch editors, paid writers, PR flacks, startups, and hacks.

When we talk about hacks, it means that this is a site where programming is involved, so as a tech recruiter, you can use this site for searching programmers specialized in R programming.

Medium is free to join, and you can sign up by connecting with Google or Facebook account, and readers can also upgrade to a membership for $5/month, giving them uninhibited access to in-depth tailored content. So, it means the same for recruiters. R programmers can help you with handling big datasets and databases, data analytics and similar.
- site:medium.com "r/programming"
- site:medium.com "r programmer"
- site:medium.com "r developer"

9. Crunchbase

Crunchbase is the leading platform for professionals to discover innovative companies, connect with the people behind them, and pursue new opportunities. There are over 55 million professionals including entrepreneurs, investors, market researchers, and salespeople.

When you use it for your recruiting purposes, connecting with the potential tech candidates is quite an easy process. When you open this platform, there is a search bar where you can add your specific keyword and search for any kind of developers or programmers. There would be a list of potential candidates that Crunchbase will show you as a searching result and you will have a direct view of important job seeker's information.

Also, this platform can give you a list of startup companies specific to your research keyword if you want to collaborate with a company in the B2B sector for example.

Crunchbase is a paid business platform, but you can use it for free too. You will be required to pay $29 per month and you will get special features for recruiting and researching too.

In the search bar, you just need to type a specific keyword for your wanted programmer, and there will be a list of potential candidates according to your searching criteria. For example, if you type Java programmer, Crunchbase will show a list of candidates matching the criteria. That's how you can connect with programmers and do your recruiting activities.

10. Behance

Behance is Adobe's social media platform for people to showcase and discover creative work. Projects that can be found there are the primary way Behance members showcase their creative work. A project is a grouping of images, text, videos, and other media that have a central theme, idea, or purpose. Each project is identified by a unique project URL that you can use to share with all of your social networks. So, that's how the graphic designers, editors, and illustrators share their work online.

Behance is like LinkedIn but for creative work and designing professionals. It's a great place to find professionals in web design, front-end development, and web development. People who want to get a job can make a profile and resume details.

You can go on Behance and sign up for an account. Next, there will be a ton of offers listed from designers and developers around the world. You can pick one, contact him/her for collaboration, and start a project together.

When you sign up for a new profile, there will be a search bar at the top where you can type a specific keyword and search for a candidate according to that criteria.

Searching examples:

- Web designer
- Front-end developer
- Remote web developer
- Short-term logo designer

After that, you can just click on any offer from the list, and the candidate's profile will appear.

Here you can see a lot of details about that candidate, including their working history, projects and portfolio, and if all of that matches your criteria, you can start your recruitment activities.

11. YCombinator

YCombinator is an American seed money startup accelerator launched in March 2005. It has been used to launch over 2,000 companies, including Stripe, Airbnb, Cruise Automation, DoorDash, Coinbase, Instacart, Dropbox, Twitch, and Reddit.

YCombinator runs two three-month funding cycles a year, one from January through March and one from June through August. YCombinator is an Investor. Now YCombinator is in some sense like any other investor. Because they're very early-stage, they're willing to accept a lot more risk than other investors are but still not a huge amount. You're very unlikely to get accepted into YCombinator with just an idea.

When we look from the recruiting aspect, with more than 2000 registered startups every year, there are always hiring activities and job seeking in YCombinator. Mostly, there are IT positions and programmers that seek a new IT job.

You just need to sign in for a new account, click the tab Startup Jobs or Internships and start your recruiting activities. There would be a list of different IT job seekers that you can contact according to your criteria.

There are different job seekers and opportunities, like: software engineers, web developers, front-end developers, back-end developers, mobile app developers, web designers, and many more.

Just pick the right one and start a conversation about your project. Contact them for details about your project, the requirements, do some testing, and make your recruiting activities flow as usual.

12. Devpost

Devpost is a platform that helps software engineers participate in software competitions. Customers market their developer tools and jobs to the Devpost community.

Devpost is like a home for hackathons. A hackathon is a tech event in which computer programmers and others involved in software development, including graphic designers, interface designers, project managers, domain experts, and others, collaborate intensively on software projects.

The candidates can sign up for an account on Devpost and participate in different hackathons that this platform is hosting. All of the hackathons are online, and big money prizes are offered for the best developers.

From the recruiting aspect, an IT candidate (software engineer, developer, programmers) can be recruited on Devpost, but key points will be missing, like: pay rate, job duties and responsibilities, experience, or education requirements.

68% of candidates who attended Devpost have looked for a job at a hackathon. While career fairs and word of mouth are the most popular ways that students look for jobs, hackathons are coming up fast. Mid-size events can bring in 100–200 students. That's a big number of potential candidates and a big opportunity for you to activate your recruiting process.

For developers, typically you can do two types of interviews: technical and behavioral. They can be live and in-person or remote via Skype, Zoom, or Hangouts. Technical interviews often include whiteboard problem solving, logic questions, pairing sessions, or even a take home exercise. That's how you can get in touch with the Devpost candidates and recruit them for your project purposes.

13. Ryze

Ryze.com is a social networking service designed to link business professionals, particularly new entrepreneurs. The site claims to have over 500,000 members in 200 countries, with over 1,000 external organizations hosting sub-networks on the site.

This business networking platform looks really simple, and all information needed is listed on the homepage. There is a free trial to sign up for a new account and get Ryzen membership, which can help you connect with new followers and potential business owners.

One of the ways to find candidates and do research about talents is to post an open job position about any IT career depending on your project purposes. That's how you can attract new potential candidates, and there is a chance to be connected with entrepreneurs for B2B collaboration.

Sign up for a new account, get a free Ryzen trial, and start to get new followers, which can be recruited by you if they match your business criteria and project requirements.

14. Scribd

Scribd is an American e-book and audiobook subscription service that includes one million titles. Scribd hosts 60 million documents on its open publishing platform. You can use this to search for users in niche industries specifically in the tech space.

Scribd is not free. However, if you are hesitating and don't want to buy a monthly membership, you can sign up for a 2-month of free trial and get unlimited access to all audiobooks and e-books, magazines, and sheet music that is available for members.

15. StackExchange

Stack Exchange is a network of question-and-answer websites on topics in diverse fields, each site covering a specific topic, where questions, answers, and users are subject to a reputation award process. The reputation system allows the sites to be self-moderating.

The Stack Exchange network of sites derives its name from its original site, Stack Overflow, but it is not the same platform.

As with Stack Overflow, StackExchange has a similar way of working, and the recruiters can connect with the potential candidates.

You can only send 100 outbound messages to candidates at any given time. However, as soon as a candidate responds to one of your messages (or if they don't respond within 7 days), you'll receive a new message credited back to your account.

There are more than 100 million users and more than 1 million job seekers and candidates for IT jobs. StackExchange Talent allows you to post listings, search candidates, and add your company page to showcase your brand. There is a Candidate Search feature that gives you the opportunity to access Stack Overflow community, which voluntarily opted in to be contacted by employers.

Annual Talent Starter package includes:

- 1 Company Page
- 1 Job Slot (with ad distribution on Stack Overflow)
- 1 user seat with Candidate Search access
- You can also purchase individual job slots.

It's highly recommended to use the premium options if you have the budget. This way you access great candidates who are highly relevant to what you're looking for. If you don't, there are ways to use Stack Overflow platform with data without allocating funds to it. There is one unbreakable rule: Adhere to policy and all will be well.

That's how you can find the most relevant tech candidates for you and do your recruiting activities as usual.

16. The Muse

The Muse is the go-to destination for the next gen workforce to research companies and careers. More than 75 million people each year trust The Muse to help them win at work, from professional advancement and skills-building to finding a job.

On this platform, you can learn what makes a company unique from the perspective of the people who work there in their own words. Also, you can chart a career with meaning, and you can find companies whose mission, vision, and values align with yours. That's a great opportunity for you to make contact for B2B collaboration.

When you open the official Muse site, there will be buttons on the top side named as "Employers" and "Jobs." Here, you can do research for your perfect candidates according to your search criteria and start a conversation with them. The Muse will give you a list according to your specific keyword with candidates, and you can choose one who is matching with your project requirements.

17. Gitshowcase.com

GitShowcase is an Open Source project designed to help developers show off their talents. If you have a profile for the project, you can help yourself by sharing it on social media and rating it on GitHub.

GitShowcase is something like a plug-and-play Github portfolio. When a developer/programmer wants to make a profile and show off their skills, signing up for a free account is a pretty easy process. They just need to open up the official website, and click the sign up button to register themselves on GitShowcase. After that, the authorization is needed to showcase the profile on GitHub, and the candidate will get an instant GitHub portfolio.

It is like a portfolio website powered by GitHub where the tech recruiters can come and search for a specific type of developer and see their skills or past projects.

That's how you can connect with the potential talents and programmers as a recruiter. The reason why the developers often choose GitShowcase is because it gives them a free hosting and their profile literally looks like a portfolio website. Recruiters often use this opportunity to easily find their wanted candidates and save time while researching.

When you open up a GitShowcase account, there is a search bar where you can type a specific keyword and set your searching criteria for your wanted developers. Let's say you can type in Java Developer, a list of Java developers will appear from the candidates that have registered GitHub accounts.

Examples of how to search Gitshowcase:

- site:gitshowcase.com "software engineer"
- site:gitshowcase.com buffalo|rochester
- site:gitshowcase.com ".NET core"

19. Dev.to

Dev.to is a community of around 570,000 amazing developers around the world. This is a place where coders share, stay up-to-date, and grow their careers. There are separate sub-pages inside the main website where the people can find different listings, videos, or podcasts.

As a recruiter, you have to know that there are thousands of developers waiting to get a job or to work for any programming project. This is a place where mostly web developers are hanging out, and they are specialized in JavaScript, Python, Java, React, PHP, and other languages.

Dev.to looks like Twitter for blogging. The programmer needs to register for a free account and become a member of the community. Then, there will be an option for all of them to create a post in the form of an article where they can inform the community members about something related to IT and coding. When the link is open, that article will appear and it is available to read.

You as a recruiter can operate the same way. Sign up on Dev.to and start posting content related to hiring programmers, web developers, or open job positions for Java developers. People who are interested will interact on your article/post, and you can establish a communication with them really easily.

Another way is to interact with people in the community who are seeking a new programming job. You can directly contact them and start your recruiting methods if you think that someone matches your project needs and requirements.

Boolean examples of how to search on Dev.to:

- site:dev.to -site:dev.to/*/* "united kingdom" javascript
- site:dev.to -site:dev.to/*/* #javascript "gmail.com"
- site:dev.to -site:dev.to/*/* "denmark" python

20. IndieHackers.com

If you are a recruiter looking to connect with IT-minded professionals, Indie Hackers may be a platform to look into. The website has been creating a buzz in the online community since its debut in 2016 and a subsequent acquisition by fin-tech company Stripe.

Indie Hackers is an online community about helping independent entrepreneurs remain profitable. It is a place where founders of profitable startups and owners of successful side projects get to share their stories. At the same time aspiring entrepreneurs have the opportunity to learn from the experiences shared. Emphasis is placed on "independent" entrepreneurs, which are those business owners earning revenue from customers rather than getting paid through an employer.

In addition, the website provides a forum setting where so-called "indie hackers" can share knowledge, explore ideas, and offer support. You as a recruiter can use this opportunity to find an "indie hacker" with specific knowledge matching your projects and requirements.

This site is something like a forum where people often write their opinions about something and engage with each other. Also, there is a section where you can navigate tabs, including community, podcast, products, and contribute where people can share their knowledge and expertise.

That's a place for you as a recruiter to start your recruiting activities. Here, people can share their stories and personal experiences where other people can engage. You can engage with someone, too, who is looking for a new job opportunity and has knowledge in programming languages, for example. That's how you can get in touch with that potential candidate and recruit him/her for your project.

Another way is to share your story here too. Write about your goals, your projects requirements, and give a powerful call to action for people who are interested. A lot of people will engage with your story, and you can choose potential candidates to start a conversation with.

Also, you can participate in forum discussions about certain topics related to your project and ask people for collaboration. That's another way for successful recruitment on IndieHackers.

21. GitLab

GitLab is a web-based DevOps lifecycle tool that provides a Git-repository manager providing wiki, issue-tracking and continuous integration, and deployment pipeline features, using an open-source license, developed by GitLab Inc.

GitLab can check your application for security vulnerabilities that may lead to unauthorized access, data leaks, or denial of service. Similar to GitHub, GitLab is a repository manager, which lets teams collaborate on code. Written in Ruby and Go, GitLab offers some similar features for issue tracking and project management as GitHub.

This is a complete DevOps platform where one application offers endless possibilities. Organizations rely on GitLab's source code management, CI/CD, security, and more to deliver software rapidly.

As a recruiter, you can sign up for a free account and do your research for GitHub repositories that match your project purposes.

In an effort to streamline the hiring process, improve the candidate experience, and hire talent faster, the best practice is to coordinate interview times, so that candidates can complete the process within 2 weeks. The initial screening call is not considered to be part of the 2-week goal. If the process before or during the team interview is taking more than a few days to confirm, you as a recruiter should reach out to the candidate, apologize, and explain what is going on.

It is a really good practice for the frequent scenarios that happen on GitLab and GitHub because of the thousands of candidates available here and the huge number of matching repositories.

Examples of how to search on GitLab:
- site:gitlab.com "software engineer" ~resume
- site:gitlab.com "Java developer" ~cv
- site:gitlab.com "web developer"

22. Javatpoint.com

Javatpoint is a well-established and popular tutorial site for learning different programming languages like Java, C, C++, and others. The tutorials include helpful illustrations, charts, and code examples, too.

Apart from that, there are different tutorials available for the site visitors, like: GIMP tutorials, Adobe Illustrator, Landing Page creation tutorials, and Javascript frameworks.

The Java section covers everything you need to know. The tutorials start with the basics of Java, discuss object-oriented paradigms, and continue to explain advanced topics such as multithreading and networking.

The best thing about Javatpoint is that the tutorials are well-structured with an easy-to-use menu system, so you can quickly find everything needed. The tutorials include helpful illustrations, charts, and code examples, too. Javatpoint also has separate sections for Android programming and popular Java frameworks such as Struts 2, Hibernate, and Spring.

As you can see, there are different sections and topics people would be interested in, and you as a recruiter can connect with them, depending on your project requirements and purposes.

All you need to do is to sign up for a free account and start your research for talents and skilled programmers. Also, you can participate in any programming tutorial on the site and get in touch with people who are participating there too. That's how you can start collaboration on a concrete project depending on the programming language.

Another way to do your recruitment processes is to use the Javatpoint search bar. This search bar is located at the top of the site, and you can type in a specific keyword to search for a specific type of programmer. Let's say you are seeking Java developers for your new project. Just go to the home page of this site and in the search bar type Java Developer.

There will be a list of Java Developers who are seeking for new opportunities, and you can choose one who most likely matches your project requirements and start the recruitment process.

That's how you can use your recruitment skills and attend new candidates for your new projects related to programming.

23. Git-Awards

Discover the top GitHub users based on City or Country across the globe.

24. Meetup.com

Meetup.com is an event based social networking site with roughly 30 million users, 300K groups, and 500K monthly meetups. Meetup can add incredible value when it comes to sourcing and recruiting talent across the globe. There's a lot of ways that you can search on Meetup.com for communities:

1. Member Search
site:meetup.com (java OR python OR ruby OR C# OR C++) "member since"

2. Member(s) Search

site:meetup.com/software/members/ (java OR python OR ruby OR C# OR C++)

3. Zip Code Search
site:meetup.com (java OR python OR ruby OR C# OR C++) 55110..554433 "member since"

4. Location State Search
site:meetup.com (java OR python OR ruby OR C# OR C++) intitle:"MN" "member since"

5. Location City Search
site:meetup.com (java OR python OR ruby OR C# OR C++) intitle:"minneapolis" "member since"

6. Network Search
site:meetup.com (java OR python OR ruby OR C# OR C++) "member since" "networks"

Group events strings examples:

- site:meetup.com "java" "meetups are scheduled"
- site:meetup.com java intitle:MN meetups are scheduled
- site:meetup.com "mobile" (kotlin OR android OR objective-c OR java) intitle:"minneapolis" "meetups are scheduled"

List string example:

- site:meetup.com "minneapolis" intitle:software (intitle:"meetup groups" intitle:meetups)

25. Bytes.com

Bytes.com is a platform that represents a community where you can connect with software developers, programmers, data engineers, and similar occupations. There are around 470,000 community members that constantly are searching for new job opportunities, have questions about different IT fields, and similar reasons. When you open up the official site, you can see that there are dozens of questions looking for answers, as well as "posts" and "topics" tabs from the menu, which can be used to search for different IT topics and be in touch with different types of IT professionals.

That's the main thing you need to remember as a recruiter when you open up bytes.com. Focus on topics which are related to your project and start answering questions in a recruiting manner. When people engage with your content on that forum, try to contact them and start your recruitment process. That's how you can be in touch with your potential candidates and activate your recruiting activities.

Examples of how to search on Bytes.com:
- site:bytes.com "software engineer"
- site:bytes.com "Java developer"
- site:bytes.com "Python data analyst"

26. HashNode

Hashnode is a free developer blogging platform that allows users to publish articles on their own domain and helps them stay connected with a global developer community.

This gives you a huge advantage: Google and other search engines send traffic directly to your domain, and Hashnode community members discover your articles on their feed. That's an awesome opportunity for you as a recruiter to hang out on the site and start your recruiting activities.

On this site, you can recruit for different positions like software engineers, programmers, web developers, and so on.

27. Kaggle.com

Kaggle allows users to find and publish data sets, explore and build models in a web-based data-science environment, work with other data scientists and machine learning engineers, and enter competitions to solve data science challenges.

You are free to copy and use them to get started on a competition. Code is available in both R and Python. Each competition has a discussion board for asking questions and up-voting kernels and topics.

The in-depth knowledge gathering is what makes Kaggle one of the most valuable platforms for aspiring and professional data scientists. The competitions can prove to be a practical learning experience for data scientists.

Kaggle has emerged as a popular platform for existing and aspiring data scientists to demonstrate their skills by solving complex problems across industries. The ability to explore collaborations to solve problems certainly makes it a big draw for companies offering short-term projects and other contract work.

Chapter 3: Creating a Talent Mapping Plan

Talent mapping is defined as researching your company's competition in relation to job openings and then using that data when you start to source candidates. You can also present this data to your hiring manager to help them understand the level of difficulty and challenge that you might face in finding candidates in certain locations.

Talent Mapping Tools:
These tools will help you monitor, track, and find leads online.

Owler - With this tool you can create custom company lists and receive news about these specific companies through the web or email.

Company Profiles
Access crucial company data, including annual revenue, employee count, location, funding history, acquisitions, recent news, and more.

Target Competitors
Meet the world's most up-to-date competitive graph in existence! Owler maps over 40 million competitive relationships between 13 million companies worldwide.

Advanced Search
Filter Owler's entire company database by annual revenue, sector, location, employee count, and public/private company status.

RANK	COMPANY	CEO		CEO RATING	EMPLOYEES	FUNDING	REVENUE
	wealthfront		Andy Rachleff President & CEO	80/100	181	$204.7M	$29M
1	**Betterment**		Jonathan Stein Co-Founder & CEO	84/100	320	$275M	$30M
2			Noah Kerner CEO	81/100	390	$255.6M	$8.7M
3	personal CAPITAL		Jay Shah President & CEO	86/100	800	$314.1M	$22.4M
4	Robinhood		Baiju Prafulkumar Bhatt Co-CEO	84/100	1,281	$1.7B	$60M

See 83 more competitors

Glassdoor - This tool can give you a valuable point of view of a company's employees. Track your competition and gain Intel on local markets.

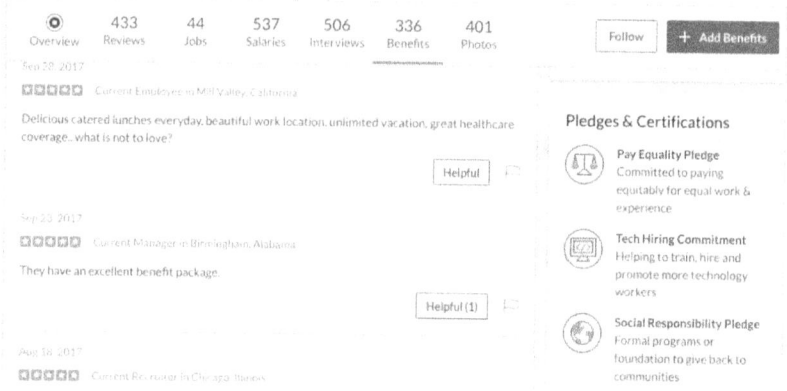

| Overview | 433 Reviews | 44 Jobs | 537 Salaries | 506 Interviews | 336 Benefits | 401 Photos |

Follow | + Add Benefits

Sep 28, 2017

☆☆☆☆☆ Current Employee in Mill Valley, California

Delicious catered lunches everyday, beautiful work location, unlimited vacation, great healthcare coverage...what is not to love?

Helpful

Sep 23, 2017

☆☆☆☆☆ Current Manager in Birmingham, Alabama

They have an excellent benefit package.

Helpful (1)

Aug 16, 2017

☆☆☆☆☆ Current Reviewer in Chicago, Illinois

Pledges & Certifications

Pay Equality Pledge
Committed to paying equitably for equal work & experience

Tech Hiring Commitment
Helping to train, hire and promote more technology workers

Social Responsibility Pledge
Formal programs or foundation to give back to communities

Chapter 4: How to Phone Screen Candidates

The first step to finding the best candidates for a job is compiling all the necessary information for the job ad. Then, once that is written and published on various job boards, the application and phone screening process begin.

It is worth considering a few key points when compiling the job ad and screening applicants. For example, in addition to listing the basic necessary skills, consider the special talents that may help weed out unqualified candidates from the start.

When assessing applications and during the interview process, be wary of the unconscious tendency to migrate towards people who share common interests or past experiences. These commonalities certainly make conversation easier, but use caution against this and other biases that sometimes hinder the hiring process. Recruiters are the gatekeepers when it comes to finding and qualifying leads. Our job is to quickly assess someone's skill sets, soft skills, and communication abilities before we schedule a technical phone screen or onsite interview.

Here, we will discuss certain details to be aware of before listing the job, as well as helpful techniques that will aid in the screening process.

1. Evaluating Resumes

The resume is basically a candidate's sales pitch to the hiring company and should make a great first impression. When evaluating the resume, look beyond matching skills and experience to the job requirements. For example, pay attention to the layout and quality of detail. Is it professionally written or does it have typos and poor sentence structure? If it's haphazardly written, it could indicate a lack of attention to detail, which may carry over into job performance. Finding spelling errors or misinformation is a red flag to reject the applicant.

2. Screening Cover Letters

The purpose of a cover letter is to make an applicant stand out above the rest. It provides an overview of who the person is, why they're interested in the job, and what they can offer. Typically, motivated candidates will routinely include a cover letter when applying for a job. If this is an important document in the screening process, make it a requirement. Have them answer certain useful questions, such as:

Why are you interested in this position?
Explain why you are the best fit for the job.
What do you hope to gain from this job if hired?

3. Assessing Video Applications

Video applications are often submitted along with a resume and cover letter. Since the goal of both the cover letter and video application is to introduce the individual and justify why they should be considered, it may also replace the cover letter. This visual tool is quite useful for asking the candidates to introduce themselves, highlight a relevant skill, and describe why they are qualified for the role, in two minutes or less.

4. Screening and Interviewing Tips

During the screening and interviewing processes, being responsive to questions and providing feedback to candidates is crucial. Even when candidates aren't suited for a specific job, making a good impression on behalf of the company is essential for both future hiring possibilities and potential references.

Interviewing Advice

You don't need to be "better" than who you're interviewing. Many interviewers suffer from the imposter syndrome, meaning they fret over whether they have the right to interview the person. They may also wonder if the candidate knows more than they do or if the candidate will see them as a fraud. Interviews aren't about superiority; they're merely a conversation about past experience.

Understand the job level: When preparing to conduct an interview, you should always review the organization's documents that explain the hiring bar and go over the necessary skills and values needed for the position. When it comes to engineering jobs, there should be a ladder that outlines the characteristics that are important for each level.

Review the technologies: Software Engineers want to know what kind of tech they'll be working with, so preparing in this regard is one of the best things you can do. You should be able to explain what technologies the candidate needs experience with and also do so in an appealing manner.

Set the Right Goals
You only have a short amount of time with the candidate, so you should be focused on the following to make the most of that time.

Gather data points that help you reach a "hire" or "do not hire" decision. Every interview should conclude with you having a clear idea of whether you may consider hiring that person and why or why not. Follow-up questions will help you get to the bottom of things to know for sure.

Sell the organization. The candidate should get a clear idea of what the organization does and why they will want to be a part of it.

Always make candidates feel good. Interviews are stressful, so never try intimidation tactics as they'll only make it harder for the candidate's true self to come through. Focus on being nice, welcoming, and informative. Candidates should leave feeling like they had a fair and professional experience.

Follow These Best Practices
If you want your interviews to go well every time, follow these best practices.

If a candidate goes off on a tangent or begins to ramble, cut them off. It's okay to take back the conversation and redirect them.
Let the candidate do most of the talking, just make sure to keep the conversation on topic.

Don't waste time with questions that any candidate could easily answer in an acceptable manner. They get you nowhere unless you're intentionally using them to try and calm a candidate's nerves.

Transcribe as much of the interview as possible and then review the conversation afterward. This will help you reconsider what was most useful to you.

At the end of the interview, you should review all your notes and use them to help form your individual decision to consider hiring them or definitely not hiring them. Rate them on a scale. From strong hire to hire or no hire to strong no hire. Don't be on the fence. Consider the facts and look at all of their technical, problem-solving, and communication skills together to come up with the right vote.

Below is a template example to use when screening an applicant over the phone:
- Are you open to looking at new opportunities?
- Have you been actively interviewing?
- What are you looking for in your next step?
- What are 2-3 elements you're looking for in your next step?
- Is there anything that interests you about our company? (Specific team, technology, etc.?)
- Are you open to the location (preference)? Would you be open to relocation?
- First off, have you connected with anyone in our company? What interests you about us?
- Have you ever worked for our company or one of its subsidiaries in the past?
- Do you now or will you in the future need immigration support to work in the US? (Please check with your HR team before asking sponsorship related questions).
    - YES: What is your current work status? Are you currently on a visa or work permit? Please specify:
- What type of work authorization do you currently hold?
    - The start and expiration date (include any extensions)
    - How long in H-1B status?

- o Do you have any green card applications pending on your behalf?
  - o Do you have an approved I-140 petition on your behalf? If so, for what position was it filed?
  - o Do you have an I-485 application pending? If so, on what date was it filed?
  - o Please list any other types of sponsorships you have held (if any), and for how long:
  - o If holding F1 sponsorship, do you hold a valid OPT EAD?
- Timeline to start?
- Without giving me any insights into your current compensation, what are your salary expectations to make a move?
- Broadly speaking, how many years do you hold in your field professionally?
- Leadership based questions:
- Tell me about a time when you saw a peer struggling and decided to step in and help.
- Tell me about a time when you didn't know what to do next or how to solve a challenging problem.
- Tell me about a time when you not only met a goal but considerably exceeded expectations.
- Tell me a little more about your current role at (company).
- What are you working on?
- Tell me about your team dynamic.

- Do you have any direct reports?
- Discuss job opening requirements and what the team/project is working on.
- End the call by talking about the next steps.

5. Phone Call Tips from a Recruiter

On average, I do roughly 10-12 phone screens per day, depending on my week. I recommend getting comfortable by using a standing desk, using a note-taking app (evernote), drinking plenty of water, and taking 10–15-minute breaks every 2-3 hours.

Let the applicants answer the questions, but don't feel bad if you have to redirect the call if they ramble on. Also, if you hear any red flags, use those hints as a way to coach the applicant during the call or afterward.

I've been doing tech phone screen calls for roughly a decade now, and the best advice that I have heard was don't feel bad if you forget a call and make sure you write everything down either in a note app or in a CRM tool. Finally, I learned how to improve my phone screens by sitting close to other senior-level recruiters on the phone. I love listening to their phone calls throughout the day. If I hear something that I like, I use that in a future call.

By implementing these screening techniques in conjunction with tools that help you optimize the process, you'll have a list of qualified candidates ready to schedule tech phone screens with your team.

Chapter 5: Boolean String Examples

Talent sourcing involves creating various Boolean strings to find profiles or resumes online. Finding resumes or profiles of candidates can be quite a difficult task.

The majority of my day revolves around searching for potential applicants. As such, mastering Boolean logic techniques is highly important in order to become an expert in talent sourcing.

I wanted to focus on one role (Software Engineer) and give Boolean string examples of how to assess search terms and then find profiles and resumes online. You can take these examples and substitute other Job titles and search term requirements.

Wikipedia defines a software engineer as a person who applies the principles of software engineering to the design, development, maintenance, testing, and evaluation of computer software. A simple way to understand the difference between Front End and Back End in development is as follows:

1. Front End Languages: HTML, CSS, Javascript
2. Back End Languages: Ruby, Python, Java, C, C#, C++, Javascript/Angular/Reat etc.

Below are Boolean string examples to find software engineers online. After understanding the differences between Front End and Back End, you can add those additional languages in your search string as well.

Searching on Social Media sites:

"i am a (senior OR lead OR sr) software (engineer OR architect OR developer)" (award OR patent OR publication OR speaker)

"I am * engineer | * developer at google" | "I am * engineer | * developer at facebook" | "I am * engineer | * developer at microsoft" | "I am * engineer | * developer at ibm"

intitle:resume site:github.* javascript engineer

site:github.com "software engineer" "joined on"

site:github.com/orgs/*/people

site:meetup.com "member since" ruby

site:stackoverflow.com/users -"Keeping a low profile." "software engineer" AND "Java"

site:com/author "software developer|engineer" "rust"

site:hackerrank.com/profile (python sql OR python nosql)
site:www.linkedin.com/in data engineer python

site:meetup.com inurl:member intitle:data.science

site:www.linkedin.com/in "* worked with * at * *" "software engineer|developer"

Resume Search Examples:

(intitle:resume OR inurl:resume OR intitle:cv OR inurl:cv OR intitle:vitae OR inurl:vitae OR intitle:"about me") (senior OR lead OR architect OR

principal) (phd OR "computer science") patent
publication –sample

site:es (intitle:resume OR inurl:resume OR intitle:cv
OR inurl:cv OR intitle:vitae OR inurl:vitae OR
intitle:"about me") (senior OR lead OR architect OR
principal) (phd OR "computer science") patent
publication –sample

(intitle:resume OR inurl:resume OR intitle:cv OR
inurl:cv OR intitle:vitae OR inurl:vitae) software
(engineer OR developer) -jobs (wa OR washington
OR seattle) (425 OR 253 OR 206)

site:slideshare.net resume "developer"

site:docs.google.com engineer javascript
site:zoominfo.com/p/ "apple inc." "developer"

site:scribd.com (CV OR Vitae) "minneapolis"
"developer"

"* * developer|engineer" (c rust OR c++ rust)
inurl:resume -inurl:pdf

(intitle:resume OR intitle:cv) ("software engineer"
OR developer) (Java OR C++) -job -jobs -sample -
examples
site:com/cv OR site:com/resume
"developer|engineer" (c rust OR c++ rust) -
stackoverflow

site:"-*-" resume "developer|engineer" (c rust OR
c++ rust) -job|jobs "gmail.com"
"resume|cv.tex at master * github" python spark
scala

inurl:resume.resume "software developer|engineer" "gmail.com"

"developer|engineer" java|python "gmail.com" inurl:resume.pdf

software (engineer|developer|programmer|architect) "view my resume" gmail.com

Resume / Generic Strings:
(intitle:resume OR inurl:resume OR intitle:cv OR inurl:cv OR intitle:vitae OR inurl:vitae)

(intitle:bio OR inurl:bio OR intitle:profile OR inurl:profile OR intitle:homepage OR inurl:homepage OR intitle:"about me" OR inurl:"about me")

(intitle:team OR inurl:team OR intitle:staff OR inurl:staff OR intitle:people OR inurl:people OR intitle:employees OR inurl:employees)

intitle:"meet*team"

(intitle:associates OR inurl:associates OR intitle:members OR inurl:members)

(intitle:alumni OR inurl:alumni OR intitle:graduates OR inurl:graduates OR intitle:alum OR inurl:alum OR intitle:grads OR inurl:grads)

(intitle:"staff directory" OR intitle:"employee directory" OR intitle:"member directory" OR intitle:"alumni directory")

inurl:meettheteam | inurl:meetourteam |
inurl:leadershipteam | inurl:executiveteam |
inurl:executiveleadership | inurl:"management
team" | inurl:"our team" | inurl:"board members"

(intitle:attendees OR inurl:attendees OR
intitle:participants OR inurl:participants OR
intitle:roster OR inurl:roster OR intitle:registrants OR
inurl:registrants)
(intitle:"resume book" OR inurl:resumebook OR
inurl:"resume book" OR inurl:resume_book)

(intitle:resume OR intitle:cv OR intitle:vitae)
(intitle:bio OR intitle:profile OR intitle:homepage OR
intitle:"about me")

(intitle:team OR intitle:staff OR intitle:people OR
intitle:employees)

(intitle:attendees OR intitle:members OR
intitle:participants OR intitle:registrants OR
intitle:roster)

(intitle:alumni OR intitle:graduates OR intitle:alum
OR intitle:grads)

(intitle:"staff directory" OR intitle:"employee
directory" OR intitle:"member directory" OR
intitle:"alumni directory")

Advanced (Software Engineer) String Examples:
(("object-oriented design" OR "ood" OR "design
patterns" OR "design pattern" OR "software design")
AND ("java" OR "python" OR "c++" OR "c#") AND
("system architecture" OR "distributed systems" OR
"algorithms" OR "subversion" OR "software
development" OR "software engineering"))

(("java" OR "python" OR "c++" OR "c#") AND ("system architecture" OR "distributed systems" OR "algorithms" OR "subversion") AND ("design patterns" OR "design pattern" OR "software design" OR "software development" OR "software engineering"))

(("system architecture" OR "distributed systems" OR "algorithms" OR "Data Structure") AND ("design patterns" OR "design pattern" OR "software design" OR "software development" OR "software engineering" OR "System Design") AND (2012 OR 2013 OR 2014 OR 2015 OR 2016 OR 2017))

(("Software Engineer" OR "Software Developer" OR "Developer" OR "Engineer" OR "Software Development Engineer" OR "SWE" OR "MTS" OR "SDE") AND ("INSERT A LIST OF TARGET COMPANIES"))

(("java" OR "python" OR "c#" OR "c++") AND ("algorithms" OR "algorithm" OR "data structures" OR "data structure")) AND ("software design" OR "software development" OR "software engineering"))

(("system architecture" OR "distributed systems" OR "distributed computing" OR "algorithms" OR "Data Structure") AND ("software design" OR "software development" OR "software engineering" OR "System Design") AND ("Senior Software Engineer" OR "Technical Lead" OR "Tech Lead" OR "Lead Engineer" OR "Lead Developer" OR "Senior Lead" OR "Principal Software Engineer" OR "Principle Engineer" OR "Senior Engineer" OR "Senior Technical Staff" OR "Principal Engineer") NOT

(Manager OR Embedded OR Mobile OR 2019 OR 2020 OR Intern OR Internship))

(("java" OR "python" OR "c++" OR "c#" OR "Ruby" OR "ood" OR "Programming") AND ("algorithms" OR "Data Structure" OR "algorithm" OR "Courses") AND (2012 OR 2013 OR 2014 OR 2016 OR 2017 OR 2018) NOT ("Senior" OR "Sr" OR "Manager" OR "Staff" OR "Principal" OR "Lead"))
((software AND design* OR architect* OR develop* AND patent AND (services OR soa OR rest OR scale* OR mongo OR nosql OR soap) AND (java OR c# OR c++ OR python OR ruby OR groovy) AND NOT (pmp OR embedded OR sas OR cobol OR as400 OR iseries OR lab126 OR audible OR imdb OR imdb.com OR faculty OR qae))

((java or C# or C++ or Python) AND ("developed" or "created" or "API" or "Microservices") AND ("SDE" or "software engineer" or "software development engineer"))

((java OR c++ OR c# OR python) AND (programmer OR engineer OR developer OR SDE) AND (algorithms OR "machine learning" OR "computer science*" OR problem*) AND (design* OR "object oriented" OR "object-oriented" OR soa OR "service oriented" OR "AWS" OR "Azure" OR "Rest" OR "web services" OR "service") AND NOT (abap OR waterfall OR embedded OR director OR pmp OR vice OR president OR ceo OR cio OR cto OR ETL OR))

Site Searching on Social Media & Community Sites:

About.me
site:about.me "Java Developer"

site:about.me | site:flavors.me "email me" software (developer|programmer|engineer|architect)

Author pages
site:com/author "software developer|engineer" "rust"

AWS
inurl:s3.amazonaws.com (cloud|iaas|paas) (engineer|developer|architect) intitle:resume OR inurl:resume

BeKnown.com
site:beknown.com "Java Developer"

Coderwall.com
site:coderwall.com "joined" "Java Developer"

Craigslist Resume
site:*.craigslist.org/*/res account "Java Developer"

Craigslist.org
site:craigslist.org inurl:res "Java Developer"

Crunchbase
site:crunchbase.com/person react redux

Dataversity
site:dataversity.net/author

Dev.to
site:dev.to intitle:dev.profile ("data science|scientist")

site:dev.to "joined on * *" "rust|rustlang"

Dev Bistro

site:devbistro.com/resumes inurl:gmail.com | inurl:yahoo.com | inurl:net | inurl:msn.com - keywords -india

Devpost.com
site:devpost.com intitle:software.portfolio.devpost

Docfoc.com
site:docfoc.com (resume OR cv OR vitae) "Java Developer"

Docstoc.com
site:docstoc.com (resume OR cv OR vitae) "Java Developer"

DoYouBuzz.com
site:doyoubuzz.com "Java Developer"

Drupal
site:drupal.org/u/ www.linkedin.com/in

Entrepreneur.com
site:entrepreneur.com/author "data science|scientist"

Facebook
site:facebook.com "Java Developer" inurl:about

Gitcoin.co
site:gitcoin.co/profile python rust

Github.com
site:github.com "joined on" "public activity" - tab.activity "Java Developer"

site:github.com "block or report" full front back "linkedin.com/in" site:github.io bitcoin "gmail.com" "developer|engineer"

site:github.com followers following "linkedin.com/in *" "rust|rustlang"

"hi|hello" "frontend|backend|fullstack" "gmail.com" site:github.io

inurl:authors site:github.com python

related:github.io.resume "software developer|engineer" "gmail.com" -"ask hn"

Google Docs
site:docs.google.com (resume OR cv OR vitae) "Java Developer"

site:docs.google.com ("hadoop" OR big.data OR "python") ("developer|engineer|architect") "gmail.com"

Gravatar.com
site:gravatar.com (resume OR cv OR vitae) "Java Developer"

HackerRank
site:hackerrank.com/profile (python sql OR python nosql)

Info
site:info (resume OR cv OR vitae) "Java Developer"

Infoq.com
site:infoq.com/profile (c++ OR java)

InnovateCV.com
site:innovatecv.com "Java Developer"

Kaggle
site:kaggle.com "data scientist" "joined * ago"
"united states"

Keybase.io
site:keybase.io ("data science|scientist")

Levo.com
site:levo.com "Java Developer"

Libraries.io
site:libraries.io "see all * * repositories"

LinkedIn Profiles
site:linkedin.com/pub | site:linkedin.com/in -inurl:dir
-inurl:title "Java Developer"

LinkedIn Resumes
site:https://www.linkedin.com (resume OR cv OR
vitae) "Java Developer"

Medium
site:medium.com/portfolio

Meetup.com
site:meetup.com "member since" Java Developer
site:medium.com (aws OR azure OR cloud architect)
inurl:followers

site:medium.com "(useState()" OR "useEffect()" OR
"unstated()" OR "useImperativeHandle()" OR
"useLayoutEffect()" OR "useDebugValue()" OR
"useContext()" OR "usereducer()"

Messari.io
site:messari.io/person fintech

site:messari.io/person bitcoin|crypto

site:messari.io/person "* analyst"

site:messari.io/person "* analytics"

site:messari.io/person "product *"

site:messari.io/person "* designer"

site:messari.io/person "frontend|backend|fullstack"

oDesk.com
site:odesk.com/o/profiles/users "Java Developer"

Pastebin
site:pastebin.com ("gmail.com" OR "yahoo.com" OR "hotmail.com") "software developer|engineer"

Resumup.com
site:resumup.com "Java Developer"

Ryze.com/go
site:ryze.com/go "Java Developer"

SCGuild.com
site:scguild.com/resume "Java Developer"

Scribd.com
site:scribd.com (resume OR cv OR vitae) "Java Developer"

StackExchange
site:unix.stackexchange.com/users

Stackoverflow.com
site:careers.stackoverflow.com "Java Developer"

StumbleUpon.com
site:stumbleupon.com/stumbler "Java Developer"

Sydex.net
site:sydex.net "Java Developer"

TalentRooster.com
site:talentrooster.com "Java Developer"

The Muse
site:themuse.com/profiles "software developer|engineer"

Twitter
site:twitter.com "Java Developer"

Uploads
inurl:wp-content/uploads github "gmail.com" intitle:resume OR
inurl:resume react redux

VisualCV.com
site:visualcv.com "Java Developer"

Visualize.me
site:vizualize.me "Java Developer"

Vimeo
"location * * * * *" site:vimeo.com software (engineer|developer|programmer|architect) "joined * * ago"

WordPress.com/cv

site:wordpress.com/cv "Java Developer"

WordPress.com/r
site:wordpress.com/resume "Java Developer"

YouTube
site:youtube.com "* is a * engineer"|"* is a *
developer"|"is a * programmer" "rust"|"rustlang"

"software engineer" "github|twitter"
site:youtube.com/*/*/about

Searching for Layoff Lists
Many candidates have been impacted by layoffs in recent months. Here's a guide on how to find layoff lists online using Boolean strings.

With so many companies furloughing and laying off employees, it's a good time to search and find active talent open for their next opportunity. As Recruiters, we are researchers, so I wanted to give some tips and tricks for finding layoff lists or announcements online. Let's use our super powers to find some great talent online! Here's some advice for finding layoff lists.

1. Search Hashtags on Social Media sites

Many leads are turning to social media during these tough times to both vent about their tough situations and even actively seek out new job opportunities. You can find these leads by using the right hashtags on platforms like Twitter, Facebook, and even Instagram. LinkedIn also supports the use of hashtags, and that's a great place to start.

When searching for hashtags, consider tags like #jobsearching, #jobseeking, #furlough, #layoffs, and so on. You can also add a location to your search, and this will help you narrow down results to your specific location, so that you can find leads more easily.

Here's an example that I found doing a hashtag search on Twitter:

The Uber and Airbnb Alumni lists published to help them find new jobs might become the new standard for mass layoffs:

Uber: https://coda.io/@kenny/uber-layoff-list

Airbnb: https://airbnb.com/d/talent

2. Set Google Alerts

There are all sorts of news coming out regarding layoffs and major changes at some of the world's biggest companies. As a Recruiter, you should stay on top of these things. So, set Google Alerts, so that you get notified whenever a new article is posted regarding job layoffs.

When you set a Google Alert, you can create it for any number of search terms. For these purposes, it's a good idea to set up Google Alerts for terms like "layoff list" and so on. Google will then notify you via email as often as you desire (a daily summary will likely be best), and you can skim the new results regularly.

3. Layoff Boolean String Examples

A Google search can reveal all sorts of helpful information, but you have to be using the right search terms just like you have to be using the right hashtags on social media. Boolean search strings on Google docs, for instance, will help you find excel lists and more that consider specific wording.

site:docs.google.com/ "layoff list*"

Doing a quick search with this string, the first doc that comes up is a Crypto Layoff list with 30+ names listed.

Another example is looking for layoff news, you can search Google news with this string: ("Laid off" OR "Layoff*" OR "Laying off"). If you're not already familiar with how to use Boolean search strings, it's worth looking into because they are major time savers. Not only can you get very specific about what results you want to see, you can get results for multiple search terms at once.

HackerNews: This is a social news website focusing on computer science and entrepreneurship.

It's a news aggregator forum site similar to Reddit, but it primarily focuses on start-ups, developers, and hacker-related news. Topics include anything that "good hackers" would find interesting. Founded by Paul Graham he wanted to create a community that would recreate the way Reddit felt in the good old days when developers were the main focus.

While reviewing the site I found out that Hacker News created a sub specifically for developers actively looking for new opportunities. This sub is a month-by-month page called: Ask HN: Who wants to be hired?

The information included in this sub:

- Name:
- Location:
- Remote:
- Willing to relocate:
- Technologies:
- Résumé/CV:
- Email:

You can create a Boolean string to find talent:

Ask HN: Who wants to be hired? ("October" OR "September" OR "November" OR "December" OR "January") AND "2019"

Roof Top Slushie: Helps you connect with employees at top tech companies like Google and Facebook. Get job interview tips, career advice, insights, and more. (Website closed down in March 2022).

Team Blind: Is an anonymous community app for the workplace. Our vision in creating this space was to break down professional barriers and hierarchy.

Google News: Is a news aggregator app developed by Google. It presents a continuous, customizable flow of articles organized from thousands of publishers and magazines.

TheLayoff: Is a site where users can list layoff updates anonymously.

Chapter 6: Talent Sourcing Tools

Talent sourcing tools are important when it comes to finding and engaging talent online. There're many tools that focus on sourcing tech talent. I wanted to highlight the top ones that most Recruiters and Sourcers recommend.

1. developerDB
This tool is a great extension to find and source tech talent online. Reach more passive candidates & sales prospects with a database of 30 million tech workers. This database consists of a wide range of tech people, many not found elsewhere, along with tech-specialized data that enables better targeting. I've had full access to this tool for a while, and I can say that I'm truly impressed by its features.
Some call outs: You can see each profile's language preferences, the contact information provided is highly accurate, and you can perform diverse searches within the platform.

Passive Candidates within the Tech Space
Reach more passive candidates & sales prospects with a large database. Find niche, hard to find candidates that would not normally be on other sites like LinkedIn or Indeed.

Traditional data providers are good at basic business information: Name, business email, job title, and company location. They are convenient as they cover broad ranges of industries but are not good for reaching tech people.
Here's why:

- There are no profiles of non-traditional tech people: ex. Freelancers, contract, or career changers.
- Traditional data is lacking deep coverage in most tech niche areas.
- No tech specific data such as tech skill rankings and "beyond work" tech activities
- Outdated information: Data is refreshed quarterly or longer.

Platform & Chrome Extension
- Find developer's tech stacks, expertise, and repositories.
- All the information needed for first contact! Users keep the data they want.
- Find the personal emails, social media, and work information online.
- Tech Rankings on various tech skills

Search on Popular Tech Sites like GitHub:

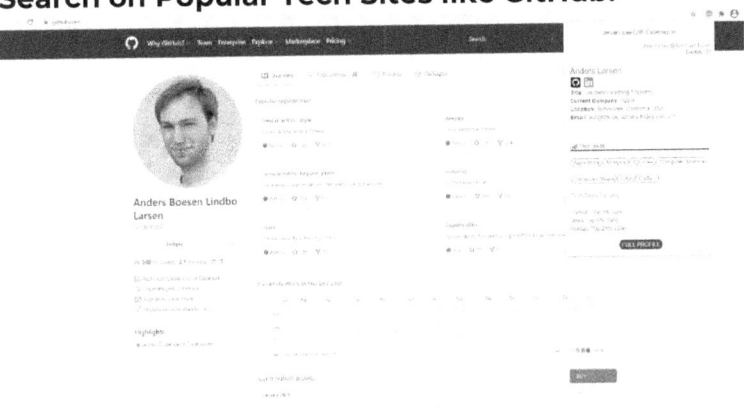

Here's What the Platform Offers:
- No credit cards required for the free trial (20 credits).
- Tech Ranking: Find top ranked talent by tech skills.
- Each profile ranks the languages that the users have used the most.
- Easy and fast: Source in minutes.

157

- Diverse search filters

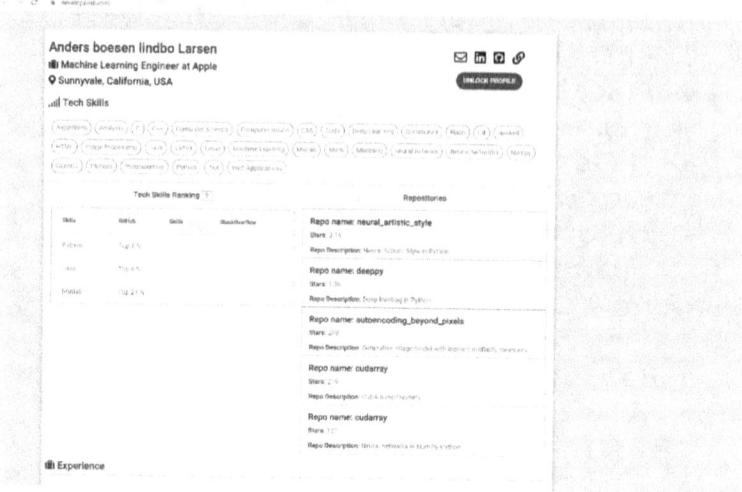

Hireflow.ai

This a new, all-in-one AI recruiting platform that helps source and engage candidates online. The tool was recently launched within the Chrome store, and I was lucky to get a quick demo from Eda Topuz. At its core, Hireflow is an AI automation tool that helps find contact information on potential leads and then it auto generates an email template message for outreach. You can easily track response rates and clicks within the tool. Overall, it's got great potential and can be used to source candidates more efficiently within LinkedIn.

1. Advanced Search AI Sourcing

- The tool learns your requirements and suggests more leads. Approve and rank profiles before you send any outreach.
- Continually learns from your feedback and improves on the search.
- Discovers the hard-to-find candidates that are missing brand name pedigree.

- Get your daily sourcing done within 5-10 minutes – 10x faster.

2. Email Outreach
- One click sourcing with the Chrome Extension.
- Automated email follow ups, personalization, response rate optimization, inbox integration, & email lookups
- The tool also integrates with many ATS/CRM tools.
- Source 3x faster and stay in your flow.

3. CRM Tracking
- Powerful data and analytics to help you focus on the right candidates.
- Collaborate with your team to keep track of candidates.
- Double response rates with nurture campaign follow ups.
- Re-engage prospects that showed interest in your email outreach but did not respond.
- Emails are optimized to send at the right time of day.

Here's what Hireflow.ai offers:
- Chrome Extension + AI Sourcing + Email Outreach Platform
- Automates the work of outbound recruiting on LinkedIn
- Finds and sends emails and follow-ups directly to your target's inbox
- Sources candidates using advanced AI semantics
- Provides diversity analytics to help you build a diverse team
- Tracks outreach and performance metrics

- All of your candidates are in one place with our ATS integration
- The free plan gives you 50 outreaches sent per month. Pro accounts start at $159 per month.

Draft and Send Messages via the Extension: Use the extension to auto populate messages based on a user LinkedIn summary info. Use the tools to send the outreach over email and track the results within the dashboard.

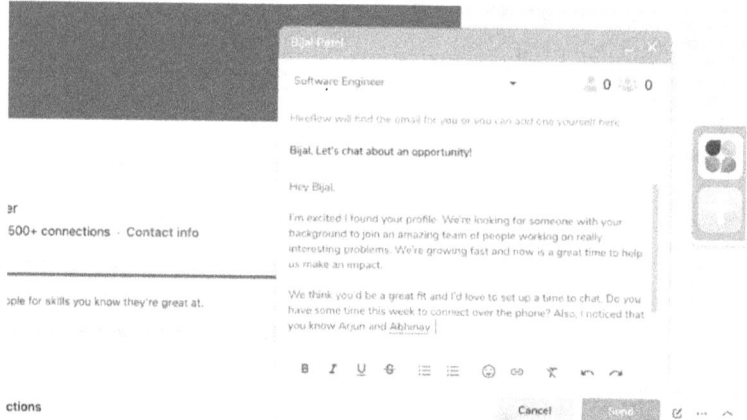

Seamless.ai

Seamless.ai is a contact finding, lead generation, and search engine tool. It encompasses many features for prospecting in sales, and it can also be used in recruiting. The tool has a search engine and CRM tool as well as a Chrome extension to help research and find leads online.

Seamless.AI claims to be the world's first and only real-time search engine for B2B contact information. "Find verified emails & direct dials, book more appointments, and win more sales!" Below is a quick overview of what Seamless offers Recruiters:

- Easily Fill Your Pipeline with Endless Leads.
- Up To 95% Accuracy – Verified in Real-Time with A.I.
- Quickly Build Lists As You Browse with our Chrome Extension.
- Over 100,000+ Sales Teams & Marketers use the tool.

1. Get Direct Access to Decision-Makers

Quickly leverage the real-time people search engine to build a massive list of decision makers or candidates. Never spend another minute scouring websites for contact information ever again. Use Seamless database to find leads for you.

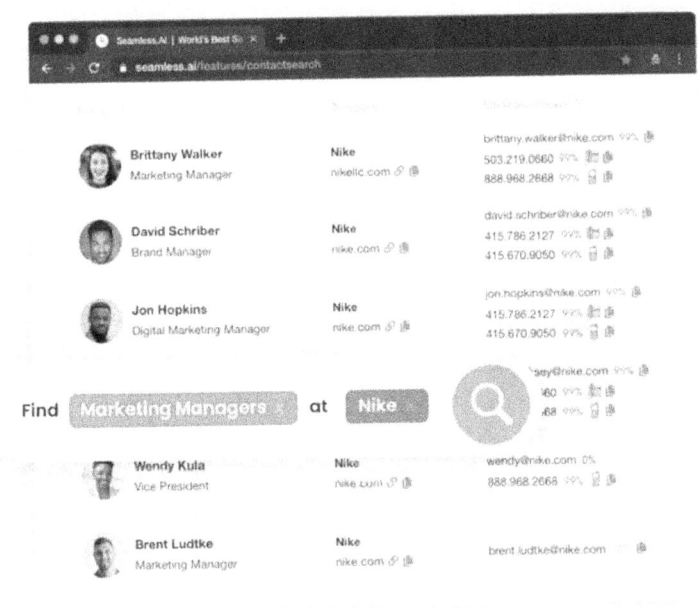

2. Find Contacts Anywhere on the Web

Quickly find all your prospect's contact information — including emails, direct dials, and more with Seamless's Chrome Extension. Turn your browser into an unlimited lead-generating machine. It helps find contact information based on a user's LinkedIn profile.

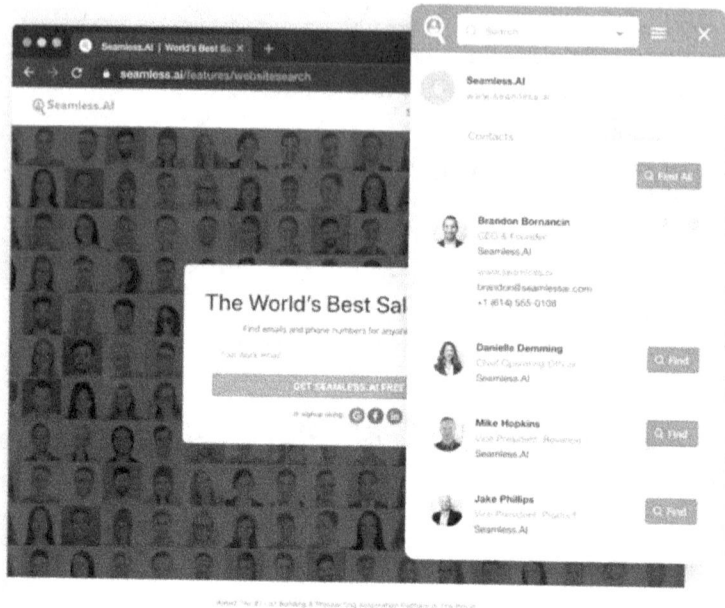

3. Instantly Build B2B Account Lists

Set filters: like industry, employee count, revenue, technology, and more — to instantly build lists from over 157 MILLION companies.

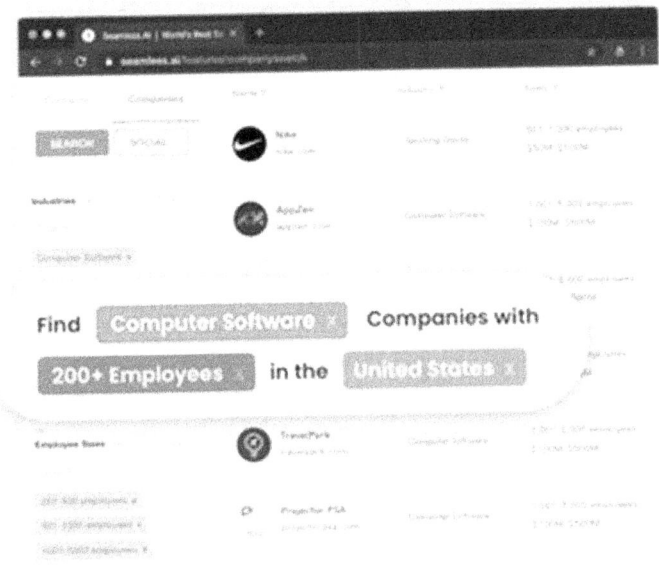

4. Use Artificial Intelligence to Find Leads

Define your ideal contact persona — with role, seniority, title or name — and get lead recommendations 24/7. Seamless uses AI intelligence to find leads based on your search requirements.

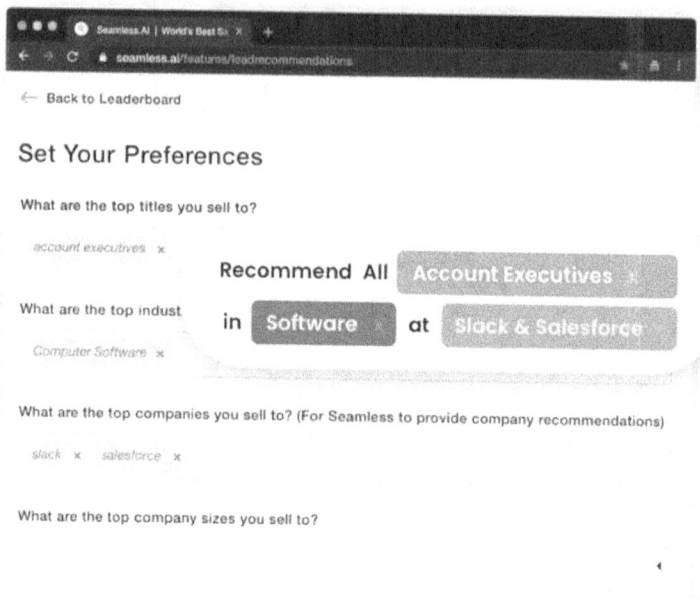

5. Know Everything about Your Prospects

Get instant pitch prep for every contact and account with customized insights. Lead conversations with what matters most to your customers. Use this intel when prospecting and engaging passive candidates.

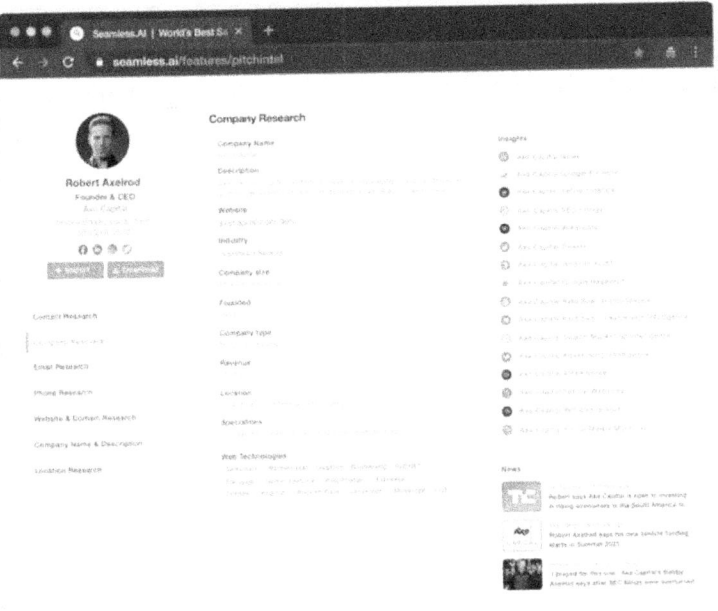

Seamless.ai is a great sales tool that can be used to find and recruit potential candidates online. I recommend getting a full demo of the tool to understand all its advanced search features.

DNNae

DNNae is a fairly new automation extension tool. It uses state of the art machine learning and AI to understand all the job requirements. It then helps you search on LinkedIn to build an active list of prospects, and finally it helps you send those leads an email or inmail message. What really makes this tool shine is that it uses AI and semantic search to help find and rank the best available talent online. It also automates the recruiter outreaches and follow ups. Overall, it's a huge time saver. On average, recruiters save 15 hours of manual LinkedIn sourcing during the work week using this tool.

Here's What the DNNae Automation Tool Offers:

- It uses state of the art machine learning and AI to understand all the skill requirements.
- Then the tool helps you search and rank candidate profiles on LinkedIn.
- All candidates are scored based on experience, skills, education, & industry experience etc.
- The candidates are sorted and rated based on job requirements.
- You can then select the prospect that you want to message.
- It will then automatically message up to 500 candidates/day WITHOUT using any inmail credits.
- All template messages are highly customizable and personalized.

How to Start a New Candidate Search:

- Click on the extension within Chrome.
- Select the candidate search.
- Copy and paste a job description or fill in the basic search requirements.
- The AI tool will then parse through the description and pull-out information.
- You will be asked to rank each experience as (Nice to Have – Important – Must Have) Skill.
- It will then request up to 1-3 LinkedIn profiles that match the requirements well.
- When you click finish you will be ready to start sourcing as off this information.

How to Add New Prospects to Your Search:

- Once you've created a new search (above), go to LinkedIn.com

- Click on the extension.
- Click on add prospects for your job.
- Once the LinkedIn search is created, click the extension and click play.
- The tool will parse and scrape each profile page.
- They recommend collecting a total of 50.
- Within the settings bar, you can select (LinkedIn on) which will allow you to use this tool in LinkedIn Recruiter.

Viewing Best Fit & Semantic Scores:
- Once you have added prospects, click on the extension and click score/connect.
- View all the prospects. Each prospect is ranked based on the semantic score.
- Semantic scores are based on the job description ranking requirements.
- Click on the semantic score to see the full detail of percentages.
- "Best fit" score compares each ideal profile's match.

Pricing Includes:
- Basic Plan: (Free)
- 10 messages per day
- Score Prospects: 1000 per month
- Premium Plan: $389 month / Billed Annually ($4668 for 1 year)
- Score Prospects: Unlimited
- Export CSV: Unlimited
- Messaging: Unlimited
- Automated Meeting Setup
- Demographic AI: Gender, Age, Ethnicity
- Best Fit Profile AI / AI Skill Match
- AI Built-in ATS with activity tracking

 DNNae

Hire Smartly.

Sign up with DNNae to automate:

Sourcing hundreds of prospects

Evaluating each of them

Reaching out to them

Setting up meetings with them

Already a User? Log In

MyRobot.Works
MyRobot.Works is a great tool to help automate your LinkedIn tasks. You can use this tool to build different talent pools and then create automated template messages to reach out to them. Overall,

it's a fantastic tool to add to your tool belt as a Sourcer!

MyRobot is designed by sales and marketing professionals, as a response to a growing need for simple, efficient and effective communication with LinkedIn connections. Personalized and authentic communication is what makes all the difference. We wanted to put a focus on the substance of our communication, on clarity and valuable content, rather than on the mechanics of delivering the message. To be able to achieve what we envisioned, we needed an automation tool to help us be more efficient. We created MyRobot.

Download the Extension (AutoMagically) to get started:
AutoMagically (for myrobot.works) makes it easy to find, attract and engage with prospects on LinkedIn. Below is what the extension tool offers:

1. Send Automated Messages on LinkedIn:
It automatically sends personalized connection requests and personalized messages on your behalf.

2. Export Connections with Email Addresses:

You can also export your LinkedIn Contacts with their email addresses. It's a browser extension which works with Google Chrome, and it will become your virtual assistant on LinkedIn – saving you hours of manual data entry when it comes to tracking all the prospects you interact with.

3. Track and Save Notes:
AutoMagically will give you leads in a lot less time. It keeps track of every single profile you visit (1st connections on LinkedIn – so people that have connected with you) and allows you to make notes directly on the profile pages, which are saved.

4. Export Profile Data:
Profile data and notes can be exported as a .CSV file to be opened in Microsoft Excel or similar tool. The file includes data such as the timestamp of the visit, name of the person whose profile you visited, job title, company name, location, email, tags, and notes. You can easily import your LinkedIn Contacts into your CRM.

Why Is MyRobotworks a Value Add for My Team?

1. Automate Your LinkedIn
Engage your audience with personalized and authentic messaging. Adapt your communication style to each pool and each individual connection. You can create templates to send an automated message to your 1st, 2nd, and 3rd degree connections.

What a like about this tool:
You can easily create a Boolean string and target profiles that fit within your search requirements. You can then create a template that auto generates

info from an individual's profile. You can then space out the reach second timing to help you to stay out of auto-bot LinkedIn jail.

2. Segment for Simplicity
Segment your network with multiple tags, for easy engagement and better results. Create pools and deliver the content that matters to the right people at the right time. Easily create a pool of possible leads and track them through your entire recruiting process.

3. Scale your Communities
Grow your network more efficiently with laser-sharp focus. Expand reach among your target audience. Use this tool to build a large network of LinkedIn connections fast and easy.

4. Synchronize Team Outreach
Eliminate the duplication of work by allowing each team member to create and manage its own pool in a shared environment. You can share your account within your teams or share profiles/pools with hiring managers.

Overall, MyRobot.Works is a powerful lead generation solution that converts your connections into an engaged audience. Reach your LinkedIn connections easier, build your network faster, engage smarter and convert more efficiently.

Hiretual (HireEz)

This AI-based recruiting platform vows to help you find and engage the right people up to 10x faster. You can source across more than 40 platforms to quickly get the information you need and get in touch with the professionals who count the most. You can outsource more than 750 million talents and their professional profiles across 30 platforms thanks to the Hiretual feature called AI sourcing assistant. This is an artificial intelligence based recruiting tool, and that is a big advantage in comparison with the competitors.

You can also use this tool for more efficient hiring across your team, looking for increased engagement and pipeline control. You can find the right people and talents 10 times faster than usual, together with their contact information to save you more time. You can get this tool as a Chrome extension and use it easily just with one click on the badge in the Chrome extensions field.

Hiretual is a paid Chrome extension, but you can start a free trial where you can get the contact finder and Boolean builder with 3 free credits per day, so you can get only 3 contacts information daily. For $79 monthly, you will get 2400 contact credits.

If you want to upgrade this package, you will get everything from this plan, plus AI sourcing, email integration on Gmail and Outlook, email templates and automation, reports and many other features. This upgraded package is called Hiretual Essentials, and you will get it for $169 per month.

If you want to use this tool, the process is really simple. You can download Hiretual as a Chrome extension. Then, you can sign up and make yourself a profile there. In the research bar just type the job name and you will get a list based on the AI sourcing feature - candidates ready for recruiting together with their contact and personal info.

Sourcing with Hiretual's AI Search

1. Start sourcing and build an open web, AI-powered search to save for a project.

2. Calibrate the AI system by selecting either 'good fit' or 'not a fit' for the populated sample candidates, then click 'Start Sourcing.'

3. Once the search runs, decide which candidates are qualified for the role ○ for those that are qualified, mark as a 'good fit' → click the candidates' name to see more profile information.

Duplicate Checking Options

This is a great feature if you worked on a large scale team. My team has Beamery, which allows us to connect and see if the applicant is already in our recruiting process. This feature is a huge time saver.

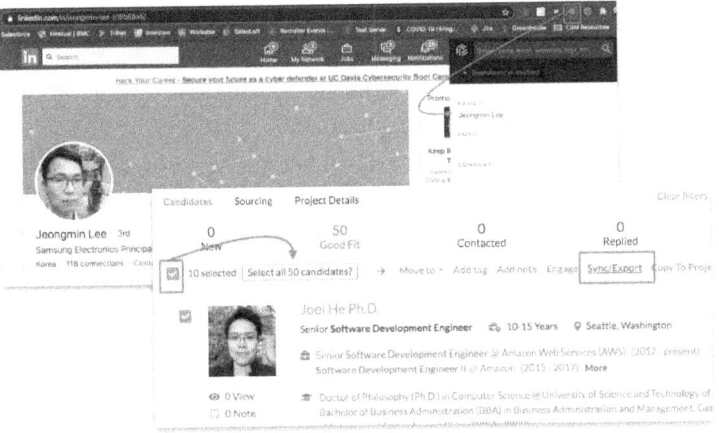

Contact Information Finding

1. Go to your preferred sourcing platform (Github, LinkedIn, indeed, etc.) and source candidate's ○ Click into candidate profile.

2. Open the Hiretual Chrome Extension.

3. You will see the candidate's full Hiretual profile, including direct contact information (email addresses and phone numbers).

4. Either add a candidate to the project in the Hiretual app or click contact information to reveal

it directly in Chrome Extension ○ Reach out to candidates directly from there, or use your preferred method of engagement.

AI Search Matching/Ranking
1. Navigate to your project, and click into your AI Sourcing task (the 'undefined search is my list of imported candidates).

2. Click 'more filters' and apply an additional filter to only look at your imported list. These candidates will be ranked, so that the candidates that most closely match the title and skill filters from the AI task will be at the top of the list. If you'd like to filter by experience, location, company, etc., apply relevant filters. This will filter out the candidates that don't match the criteria.

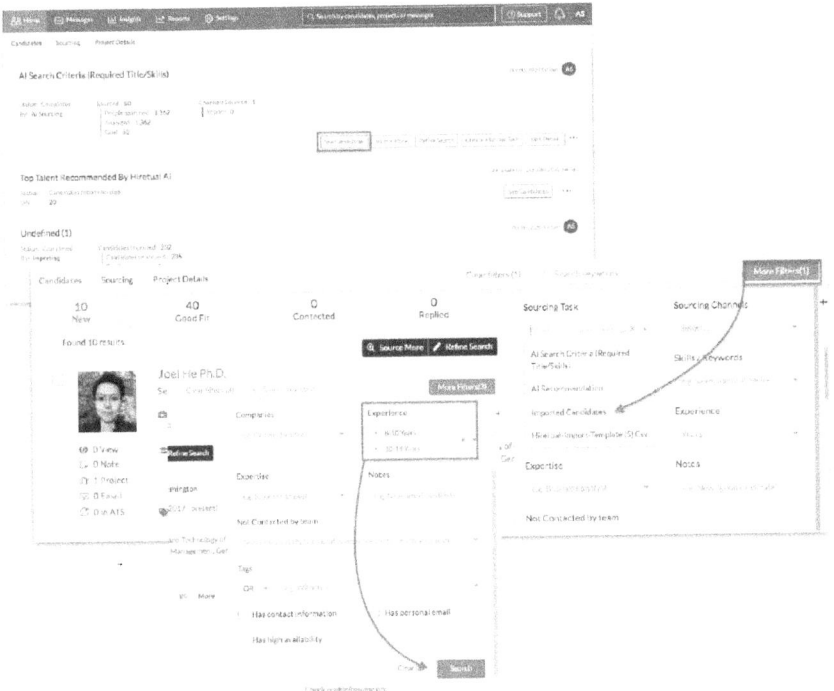

Selecting Leads that Meet Your Search Criteria

1. Once you finish applying the filters, decide which candidates meet your criteria. For those that are qualified, mark as a 'good fit' → click the candidate's name to see more profile information.

2. Export Candidates in CSV file from 'Good Fit' stage in Hiretual.

3. Use contact information in CSV files to reach out to candidates using preferred engagement methods.

Outreach Email Sequence Campaigns

1. Simply create a project and advance these leads to the email campaign sequence stage.
2. Create sequences with recruiter templates.
3. Track each sequence and follow up. See who opened and clicked on each message.
4. You can message someone up to 10 times within the tool.

Expanded Search on Google

When doing searches on Google, you can now see a full profile of an individual.

SeekOut

SeekOut has a comprehensive database and offers access to an intuitive AI search that covers whole person profiles. You can also engage professionals across industries and use personalized messaging tools for the best results. This tool is a powerful AI search engine that recruiters love to use for instant contact information and personal profiles collecting.

I've been able to speak with their co-founder Anoop on several occasions. I've been very impressed by this extension and everything that you can do with this platform.

This tool has amazing features, some of which can be used to extract and organize candidates and talents. Here, you are allowed to search for the complete and verified profiles on LinkedIn and Github and sort the candidates by project needs. Next, there is a feature where you can export the candidates' list in CSV files, so you can easily check the list up and choose the right candidates for pitching.

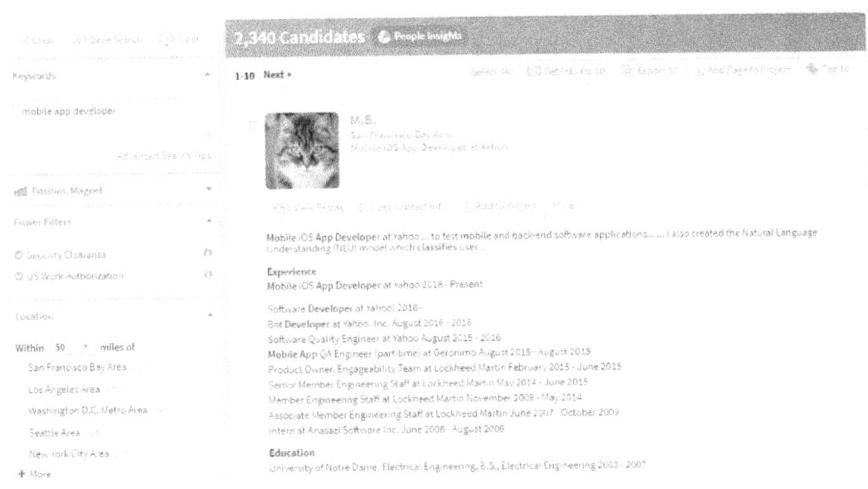

Here's all the Seekout Features:

A large vast pool of Talent:

Talent Pools	Description	Great for Hiring	Number of Profiles	Availability
Public Profiles	Candidates' professional experience, education, and skills from public profiles	All roles	440M+	All SeekOut licenses
GitHub Profiles	Candidates' overall coding expertise and experience with specific programming languages based on analyzing their code and contributions to Open Source projects	Software Engineers	25M+	Premium Tech licenses
Expert Profiles	Candidates' deep subject matter expertise based on published papers, patents, conferences, as well as metrics which measure how frequently a candidate is cited among papers	Deep subject matter experts in technical fields including engineering, pharmaceuticals, economics, and machine learning	85M+	Expert licenses
Candidates in your ATS	Rediscover warm candidates from your ATS or CRM based on SeekOut's powerful search of their current profile	Great candidates that have previously applied to your company	Varies	Requires integration. Contact your SeekOut representative for details.
Employee Referrals	Identify candidates connected to your employees and easily request feedback on potential candidates directly in SeekOut	Employee Referrals	Varies	Contact your Customer Success Manager for details
37 other social and professional networks	Custom search across 37 different social, professional and technical sites from Facebook to Kaggle and more	Candidates who don't typically have professional public profiles, such as nurses, retail workers, and commercial drivers	Varies	All SeekOut licenses

AI Searching

With SeekOut's AI-Powered Talent Search Engine, you can search the way you want to find the candidates you need. Use machine learning and AI to find candidates who match the requirements for any job description.

Search Methods	Description	Example	Availability
Direct Search	Fast, accurate results based on keywords	Java developer Seattle	All SeekOut licenses
Boolean Search	Full Boolean support, powerful field-based syntax, wildcards, and more to build targeted, highly precise searches	our _title ((radio OR antenna) AND engineer) AND (frequen* OR design)	All SeekOut licenses
Power Filters	Over 300 complex queries for in-demand roles available with a single click	☑ Front-end Frameworks ☑ MachineLearning	All SeekOut licenses
AI Matching	Automatically find great candidates that match your job descriptions	Find best fit candidates from any JD	All SeekOut licenses
Diversity Search Filters	Take actionable, specific steps to improve diversity in your organization by finding and including highly qualified, diverse candidates in your recruiting pipeline	Search filters for female, Hispanic, Black or African American, and veteran candidates	All SeekOut licenses
Enhanced Clearance Filters	5 times more cleared candidate search results than any other tool, with the industry's most precise control over clearance level searches	12 precise levels of clearance and access filtering	Expert Licenses, or Premium Tech Licenses with Enhanced Clearance Filters upgrade. Requires activation. Contact your SeekOut representative for details
Custom Power Filters	Custom Power Filters designed to improve your team's efficiency and meet the specific recruiting needs of your organization	Custom	Speak with your Customer Success Manager to understand available options for Custom Power Filters

Talent Pool Insights

Analyze the frequency or scarcity of specific skill sets and backgrounds, the geographic distribution of talent, and where candidates currently and previously worked. Use these insights to build an actionable recruiting strategy, benchmark against your competition, and more.

Engage Candidates

Contact candidates using highly verified phone numbers and emails and improve candidate response rate with automated, integrated, and personalized email engagement.

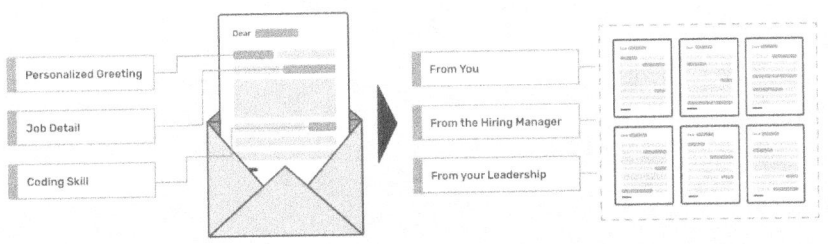

Find Highly Qualified, Diverse Candidates

Take action to improve diversity in your organization by finding and including highly qualified, diverse candidates in your recruiting pipelines. SeekOut's diversity search filters for female, Hispanic, Black or African American, and veteran candidates deliver up to five times as many highly qualified diverse candidates as other recruiting tools.

Expanded Search on Google

When conducting a search, Seekout will expand individual profiles.

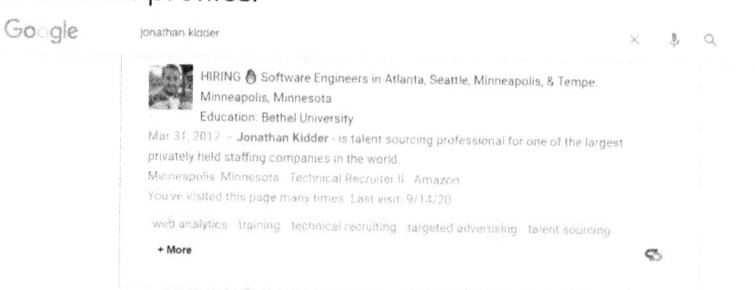

Within each profile, there will be keyword tags. Scroll over each keyword to get a definition. This will help improve your sourcing abilities.

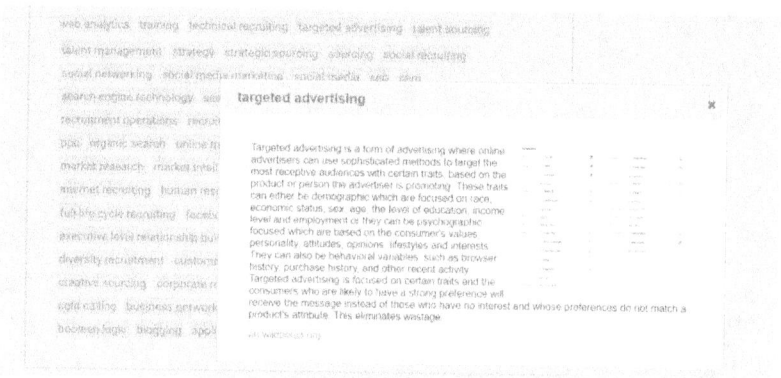

HiringSolved

This is award-winning AI recruiting software that helps professional recruiters with amazing workflow and team focus in the process of talents searching. Using this tool, you can upgrade your team productivity and automate some processes like sourcing and outsourcing, engaging and similar processes, and retaining the right candidate for your business needs no matter how much time you want to contract them.

Using HiringSolved, you can get a lot of features, including the availability to unify HR data. This feature will allow you to unify CRM, HRIS, and ATS with one search interface. There will be real time business insights too, so your wanted candidates will be perfectly matched with their job experiences.

Also, this tool is offering automation processes where the recruiting team can easily connect and focus on the workflow as well as the human steps during the recruiting process. The historical hiring trends and market insights can be supervised live, so that's how you will benefit from looking for the right people at the right time.

HiringSolved is a recruiting tool based on AI, so you just need to sign up on their official site and make yourself an account. Then just search for a specific keyword or job description, and the list of potential candidates will appear on the screen, together with their info.

Hired
The team at Vettery/Hired attracts and engages candidates to sign up for this platform. They only allow candidates who are "actively open" to a new role to join. The majority of the candidates are mid to senior level with an average of 6+ years of

professional experience. The platform does not focus on bootcamp or entry level candidates.

They have roughly 90K active users within the platform and continuously add new leads every Monday morning. They are currently in over 22 cities across the globe. Overall, their leads are primarily in the Tech, Finance, and Sales space.

Hired offers a hiring solution that is up to 4X faster than job boards, passive sourcing tools, and staffing agencies with their:

- 1000+ new vetted candidates added weekly for quality and intent
- 100% candidate response rate in 72 business hours
- 60% interview acceptance rate
- 75% offer acceptance rate

Advanced Search Features:

- Easily create a role and search for candidates using intuitive filters.
- You can list out additional requirements within a search.
- AND/OR Boolean searching features.
- Search for leads who have expressed interest in your company.
- Search for leads willing to relocate or work remotely.

Diversity Partnerships

The team has partnered with many tech related BLNA networks including #HIREBLACK (a global organization that is aiming to place and promote 10,000 Black women by 2021), Girls Who Code, Year Up, Dress for Success, TechNYC Summer Bridge, and Hired's sister company General Assembly (a global leader in reskilling talent, to help drive increased diversity). In a whitepaper recently released by Hired, they outline how remote work can promote diversity and inclusion in the workplace, as well as how to easily source for remote candidates using Hired's "Remote" toggle.

Here's what I like about this tool:
- Candidates are required to respond within 3 days.
- Easily integrate your calendar with Gmail and Outlook.
- Once a profile responds, they have to auto schedule a time to speak with you! No back and forth compared to other platforms.
- Add notes on profiles and easily tag a profile for further review from an HM or team member.
- If another team member reaches out, you cannot reach out as well.
- Easily integrate into your ATS system. They currently connect with Greenhouse and Lever automatically.

Additional Questions that the team answered for me:

1. What cities does Hired work in?
Hired candidates are based in the U.S., Canada, Ireland, and the U.K., and many are open to remote opportunities. Candidates indicate their preferences, so hiring managers can filter accordingly.

2. Is Hired a staffing agency?
No. Staffing agencies essentially act as a broker between you and the candidate. Hired is a hiring marketplace. We create transparency between you and the candidate by bringing active employers

and active candidates to the same place and allowing you to reach out to them directly.

3. What does Hired cost to use?

It has three pricing models:

1. Starter Plan – No up-front commitment, no access fee. Best for ad hoc hiring needs and small teams. The fee for a single placement is 15% of the candidate's first-year salary.

2. Premium Plan – Small access fee, reduced hiring fees. Best for teams with limited hiring needs. The fee for a single placement is 10% of the candidate's first-year salary.

3. Unlimited Plan – Yearly contract with zero hiring fees! Best for large or growing teams with constant hiring needs.

There are several other companies that provide comparable candidate searching platforms. However, Hired stands out due to its incorporation of features such as ATS integration, calendar scheduling, and diversity sourcing options, which are not taken into account by other platforms.

OctoHR

OctoHR is a tool used on GitHub profile pages for Recruiters. Helps recruiters to get more information about developers. It simplifies search for the new candidates in GitHub. It's a great way to understand what types of coding language a user has experience in.

EmailOnGitHub

EmailOnGitHub Chrome extension allows you to discover info associated with a user's GitHub profile.

- Once installed, go to GitHub -> user's info (email and if user is available for hire) will be displayed right under user's login (see photos attached) – if no email is found, you'll see message "email not found"
- Current version allows you to check 30 GitHub user's profiles per hour (they will be working on increasing this number).
- They advise you to be logged in your GitHub account and use Chrome browser for better results (if you don't have a GitHub account, you can create it for free).

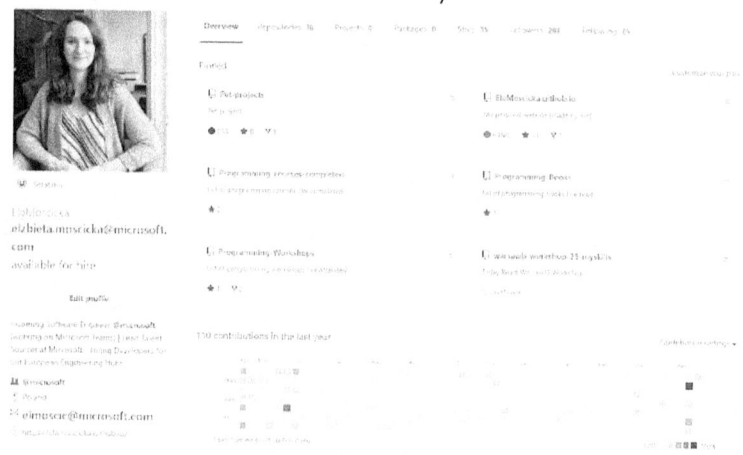

GlossaryTech

This app allows users to quickly see definitions of tech-related keywords. I've used this app to quickly understand different types of tech skill sets.

In the past, when searching on Linkedin or Github profiles, there were certain keywords that I would have to research further on Wikipedia or Google. This caused me to lose valuable time throughout my week to research and understand other keywords.

Also, it was good to understand other keywords that correlated with what I was searching for. I've been talent sourcing for over 8 years now, and in order to source and qualify applicants better, you really need to understand the field that you're sourcing in. So, having an app extension like GlossaryTech is really invaluable to my success as a Talent Sourcer.
You can use this extension on sites like: LinkedIn, GitHub, or StackOverflow.

Here's What It Actually Does:
- Detects and highlights technology terms on a web page just in a few seconds
- Provides their easy-to-understand definitions in a small overlay
- Filter found tech terms by category (Front-end, Back-end, QA, etc.). Each category has its own color

How to Get Started:
- Once you download the extension, create a free account login.
- Do a simple Boolean string search on LinkedIn.
- Hover your mouse over highlighted terms to see their descriptions.
- To filter the terms by category, use the sidebar. For this, just click the icon in the ribbon. Each category has its own color.

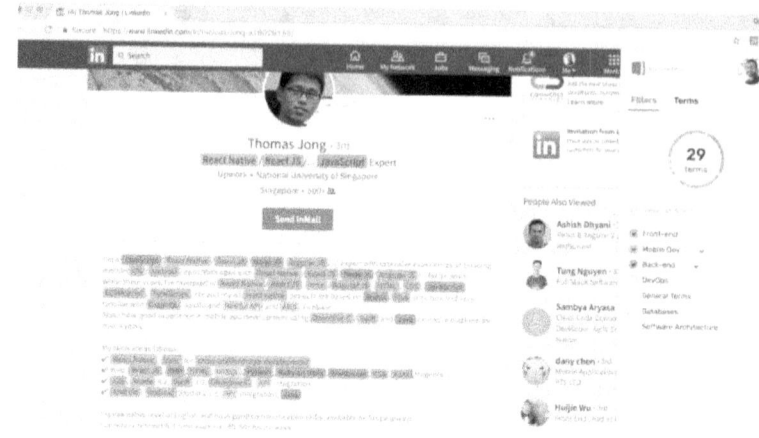

RecruiterWand

WizardSourcer has created a browser extension called Recruiter Wand. This free extension will allow the user to create auto-filled emails for contacts on LinkedIn or other social media platforms. The extension will capture the names, company, and skills on the page and auto fills them into a template. The user can choose from a list of pre-saved templates. You can add additional templates within the tool as well. The user can then copy the autogenerated text and paste it into emails and other messaging platforms.

This tool was created out of frustration with filling in email templates for my recruiting messages.

What are the benefits to using this tool?
1. It's a free way to manage recruiter templates all in one place.

2. Select from a large variety of auto filled templates in many different industries.
3. Add and save additional recruiter templates within the tool.
4. Auto fill in templates with the applicant's most updated information.
5. Speed up sourcing and messaging abilities.
6. It's simple and easy to understand and use.

How to use this extension tool?
1. Download the extension in the Google Chrome store.
2. Search on LinkedIn or one a website page with resume details.
3. Select the Recruit Wand tool to load in the Chrome browser.
4. Then go to a candidates LinkedIn profile, select (Get LinkedIn Data), and auto fill in the template.
5. Include a date of availability – easily give your availability for that day or week.
6. Once you've auto filled in the template, select copy and then paste it into an email or inmail.

Chapter 7: Best Practices for Sending Messages

Crafting a perfect recruiter message takes time. In order to engage and get a response from a diverse lead, you will need to understand the fundamentals of creating an email or inmail message. Below, I will walk you through examples.

Note: These examples would work best in North American markets only. The European market is quite different when it comes to messaging candidates online.

Looking to write the perfect recruiting cold call email? There are six elements you should consider critical when writing an email to a passive candidate. Recruiters need to spend the time to craft a message that is unique and personalized for each lead. You will only have a few seconds before that lead is either responding or sending your email to the trash bin.

1. The Subject Line

Keep your subject line under 3-4 characters to make sure mobile users can read it. Remember, your subject line determines whether or not your prospect will actually open and read your message. Try to appeal to their ego, and you'll give them a "mini high" that will have them wanting more.

2. Paragraph I

The first "paragraph" should really only be a few sentences long. You should warm them up by starting off with an explanation of how you reached out to them specifically with this role in mind. Tell them how you found them, too. You should be working to prove that you did your homework. Share their blog, portfolio, social media profiles within this first paragraph. Try and pull them in with your interest.

3. Paragraph II
In the second paragraph, you need to tell the prospect what they want to know about the role you're offering up. They mainly want to hear about a career trajectory, the expectations of the role, and the responsibilities they'd be taking on. Be honest about the workload and walk them through a "day in the life" in this position. According to LinkedIn, this is what candidates want to know the most. They want to understand the project or team and what they are trying to accomplish.

4. Paragraph III
In your third paragraph, you should touch on your Employee Value Proposition, or EVP. That means covering the unique benefits the prospect would get to enjoy as an employee of your company. Make sure you frame these benefits as perks that they'll get in exchange for bringing their unique skills and experience to the company. That way you continue to make them feel good about what they have to offer.

EVP might include discussing how there are no product managers, meaning they'll get to drive the product development from beginning to end. You might also point out all the growth opportunities they'll have in front of them as you expand your team to double or triple in size in the next year. Talk about the flexibility of the environment and other things they'll enjoy. An example for us is that we've gone fully remote – that's a huge plus for candidates during this time.

5. The Call to Action
Your call to action, or CTA, is all about getting your prospect on the phone. If you can do that, you've achieved your goal. Your CTA should be short and friendly, just like the rest of your email. Some people employ the strategy of telling the prospect when they'll call, like saying: "I'll try to catch you on the phone this Friday at noon", or you can take a more traditional approach and offer them to connect. Be sure to keep your CTA cool and casual. This is a friendly conversation, not a sales pitch–or, at least, that's how it should feel.

Using humor has helped me to get leads to respond: sending a meme or picture of my dog has paid off many times. The point is try and use creative ways to encourage them to respond.

6. The Signature
Your signature is critical because that's where your prospect will look to find your contact info and anything else they need to know to get in touch with you. Then leave your number as well. This is how they'll be able to reach out to you now that your cold call email has sold them on the idea. I like to bold my cell number and include my time zone.

7. Personalization & Uniqueness Get Responses
Whenever reaching out to a candidate, be personalized and avoid using generic templates. Take the job out of the conversation, do not start the message or email by saying you have an opportunity. Always start the message mentioning

something specific about the candidate and what made you want to reach out? Having 10 people respond from 20 reach out messages is far more efficient than sending out 100 messages and still only 10 responses.

Whenever reaching out to candidates, keep the following in mind:
- Unique & Creative subject lines!
- Personalized Content
- Aim for > 50% response rate
- Keep the word count to under 500 characters
- Is your message optimized for reading it on a mobile device?
- Keep sentences short.
- Free of spelling & grammatical errors (Download and use Grammarly)
- Include questions and call for action.
- The LARGER the volume per batch of reach outs, the LOWER the response rate
- Never let a response go to waste – set up future touch points.
- Memes, gifs, pictures, or emojis work to cause a positive reaction

The right subject line is the secret to an effective recruiting email, so why do most people spend just mere seconds writing one when they can spend an hour or more creating the email itself? If you're doing things right, you'll spend at least as much time considering your subject line as you do your email's content because, after all, if the subject line isn't an attention-grabber, the rest of the email will never be seen anyway.

Of course, it can be tough to come up with a succinct and engaging subject line, especially for recruiting emails. To help you out, here are some ideas you can use, ranging from funny to those that provoke curiosity or a fear of missing out (FOMO), so that you can get more opens and, ultimately, more responses.

Here's the Best Recruiting Email Subject Lines I have found online:

Make Them Laugh
A clever subject line can certainly grab a candidate's attention. Take these, for example...
- Seeking a Tiger King, Carole Baskin need not Apply
- I tried calling earlier but got crickets
- Re:re:re:re:re:re:re:My Last Follow Up
- We're Still Hiring During the Apocalypse

Provoke FOMO
"Fear of Missing Out" comes from a candidate realizing how great an opportunity is. These subject lines help provoke this sensation...
- Matthew, I'm Building An Avengers Marketing Team
- This Job Is Better Than a Friday Night at [Popular Bar Near Prospect's College]
- Let me introduce you to a better opportunity, Matthew.
- How's 2020 Starting at [Company]?
- We have Zoom Parties on Fridays

Entice Curiosity
Get them thinking about a position's potential with one of these enticing subject line examples...
- Matthew, Picture Yourself Creating [product] at [company name]
- Have you heard about [company name]'s upcoming launch?
- Your resume caught my interest, Matthew!

- Who's the worst boss you ever worked for, Matthew?
- What's the best job you ever had, Matthew?

Be Friendly in Your Follow-Up

Follow-up requires unique personalization to spark a conversation. Take a look at these examples.

- How's your job at [current company] going?
- Can we talk about your boring job, Matthew?
- Let's have a convo about your future.
- Want to grab a coffee with me next week?
- Do you have time for a chat about your career?
- I Just Left You a Voicemail

Dealing with a Crisis

What are their current needs? What are their current circumstances? Are your prospects stuck at home? Are they dealing with taking care of their children or finding ways to continue their education during quarantine? Are they trying to provide for family members at high risk? It's good to factor in these thoughts into your subject line when reaching out to passive applicants.

- Matthew, I'm just checking in with you
- How's work been at [company]?
- We're GROWING under uncertainty

Best Practices

As you read through these examples and search for inspiration to craft your own recruiting subject lines, don't forget about the best practices surrounding writing the best subject lines.

In general, the most engaging subject lines are between 61 and 70 characters long. You should tweak your subject line until you get it to this range, always remembering to keep things succinct. Every word counts in such a short string of letters, so come up with multiple versions and pick the one you think gets your point across best.

Remember, your subject line is only the introduction to your email. You don't have to say it all in the subject line, and there's no way you could. Rather, try to get the most important idea across in your subject line. so that the person actually cares to open up the email and see what it's all about.

Finally, make sure that your subject line ties into the rest of the email. The first one or two lines of the email need to capture their attention just like the subject line did in order to pull them in, so they read the whole thing. Your subject line should be relevant to what you're saying in the email – no click baiting!

Here's a clever message to send to Software Developer:
https://wizardsourcer.com/a-clever-way-to-message-software-developers-about-opportunities/

```
Def __init__(self):
Self.title = 'Next career move'
Self.looking_fob_job = true
Self.not_interested_now = true
Def _if_looking_for_job(self):
If self.looking_for_job:
Self._apply_job(self,job_id)

Else:
Print('Thank you for looking at my email. Save my contact for future purposes. Have a good day J ')
Def _if_not_interested_now(self):
```

```
If self.not_interested_now:
Print('Please refer someone whom you think can
match your expertise')
Self._save_my_contact_info()

Else:
#if mind change and wanted to apply
Self._if_looking_for_job()
Def _save_my_conatct_info(Self):
# contact info
Print ('Jonathan – 651-792-5869 –
jonkidde@amazon.com')
Def _apply_for_job(self,job_id):
# review job description here, click and respond
Print('Inset Job Description Link Here")
```

Using Binary to Send Messages to Developers

I've discovered a creative way to engage with developers online using Binary convert to text methods. Using this site called RapidTables, you can add messages and convert them into Binary code. The binary system is used by almost all modern computers and computer-based devices. So, it's definitely a great way to talk nerd to a developer! For example:

Please email or call me here:

00110110 00110101 00110001 00101101 00110111 00111001
00110010 00101101 00110101 00111000 00110110
00111001 00001010 01101010 01101111 01101110 00101110
01101011 01101001 01100100 01100100 01100101
01000000 01100001 01101101 01100001 01111010 01101111
01101110 00101110 01100011 01101111 01101101 00100000

I've had a few good laughs with other developers when they see this message on a LinkedIn profile.

You can also start to play around with this in other recruiter messages in email and inmail.
It's a fun creative way to engage with developers online!

How to Use Mail Merge to Recruit Candidates

As a Recruiter, outreach and follow-up are at the core of your position, but they both involve a lot of tedious, manual, monotonous labor in order to do it right. Fortunately, lots of "secret" tools are out there that could help take away some of that touch work. Mail merge from Microsoft Word or Excel is one excellent example.

What is mail merge?
Looking to customize a document, such as an email or newsletter? A mail merge is the answer. With a mail merge, you can instantly and automatically personalize any number of documents for all of your recipients, sparing you lots of manual labor.

For instance, if you're sending cold emails, you can use a mail merge to add a unique greeting, mention each candidate's name, and even include their job position, company, and other relevant details. That means you just need to type up a template first, and a mail merge will instantly insert all their info from a spreadsheet. In other words, it's a massive time saver.

How to Use Mail Merges

The first step to using mail merge is getting the two components setup. The first is the template file, which is the document you send out (such as your email) with the placeholders where you want to insert the personalized data and the second is the data file, which is a Microsoft Excel spreadsheet or Google Sheets file where you organize the personalization data.

When you open your template file in Word or Excel and navigate to the Mail Merge feature, it will prompt you to select the location of your data file, and it will do the rest of the work for you, filling in the placeholders of your template with the data for each recipient and generating a personalized email or letter for everyone in your list.

What: Mail Merge is the process of compiling a list of a large amount of contacts that you want to email all at once instead of one at a time. You are able to somewhat personalize your messaging with a mail merge which is highly recommended as you do not want to come off as spamming candidates.

Preliminary Work: Compile a list of all of the candidate's information you want to reach out to in excel. You must include first name and email at a minimum, but you may add other personalized filters such as current company, skill set, location, etc.

Example:

	A	B	C
1	**First Name**	**Email**	**Company**
2	Vegas	vegas.miller@gmail.com	Leidos
3	Nathan	natem559@gmail.com	Hollstadt
4	Vaishali	vaishalikumar@hotmail.com	Lifetouch
5	Callie	callie.f.bensel@gmail.com	Upsie
6	Thomas	thomasohagen@gmail.com	Optum
7	Joseph	jwitthuhn@uwalumni.com	Thomson Reuters
8	John	jhnkotz@gmail.com	SmartThings
9	Jacob	jacobrdalton@gmail.com	Sentera
10	Charles	chajohnson10@gmail.com	Express Scripts
11	Michael	mpcitak@gmail.com	IDeaS Revenue
12	Nicholas	boldt.nicholas@gmail.com	NextEra Analytics
13	Chad	cmrobinson@gmail.com	Virtuwell
14	Joseph	jayr86@gmail.com	Target

Step 1: Once you have all of the candidates you wish to email in your excel spreadsheet, save the document and open Microsoft Word. Insert the template you wish to use for the body of your email and add in the column names where your personalized information will go (name, company, etc.)

Once complete, on the top click "Mailings" and then "Start Mail Merge" and then from the drop down hit

"Step-by-Step Mail Merge Wizard." Once you hit "Step-by-Step Mail Merge Wizard", a column titled "Mail Merge" will appear on the right-hand side. Click "Email messages" and then click (step 1 of 6) "Next: Starting document" at the bottom of the screen.

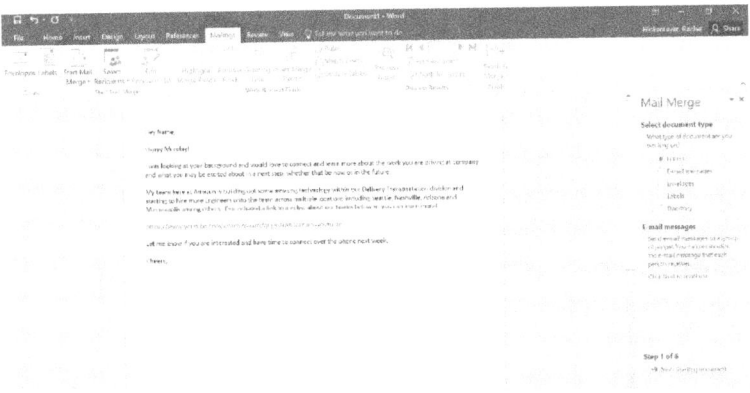

Step 2: Click (step 2 of 6) "Next: Select recipients" at the bottom right.

Next, click "Use an existing list" and then hit "Browse" to find and double click the Excel document with the contact information you compiled initially.

Once you double click your document, a window titled "Select Table" will pop up. Click "OK."

Next, another widow will pop up titled "Mail Merge Recipients". Assure the column headers are correct (Name, Company, Email, etc.) and then click "OK."

Step 3: On the bottom right of the screen (Step 3 of 6), click "Next: Write your email message".

Under "Write your email message", click "Greeting line…" A window titled "Insert Greeting Line" will then pop up where you can choose your preferences. Because in the example template "Hey" is already included as the greeting and a comma is also already included after "Name", I will choose "(none)" for both of these options in addition to "Greeting line for invalid recipient names". For the person's name, I chose the full name "Joshua."

After you have these selections made BEFORE you hit OK, click on "Match Fields."

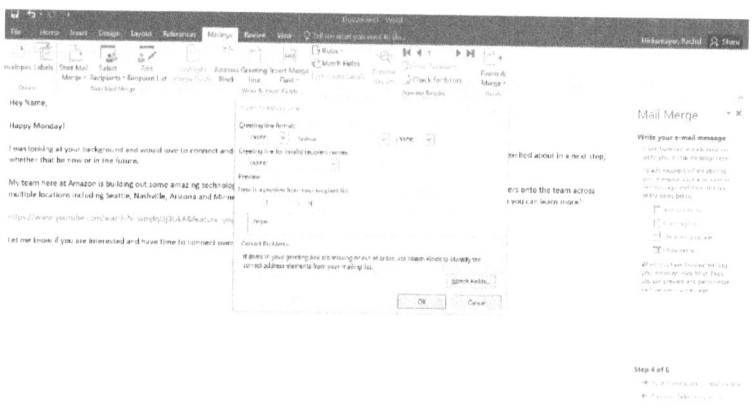

Once you hit Match Fields, a window will pop up titled "Match Fields." This is a very important step to ensure the fields in your excel spreadsheet convert over accurately to the Word doc template (in this example we would be looking to make sure name, company, and email match). Check all personalized fields to assure the columns on the left hand side and match the ones on the right which represent your excel sheet. Scroll down to assure the email matches as well. Hit "OK."

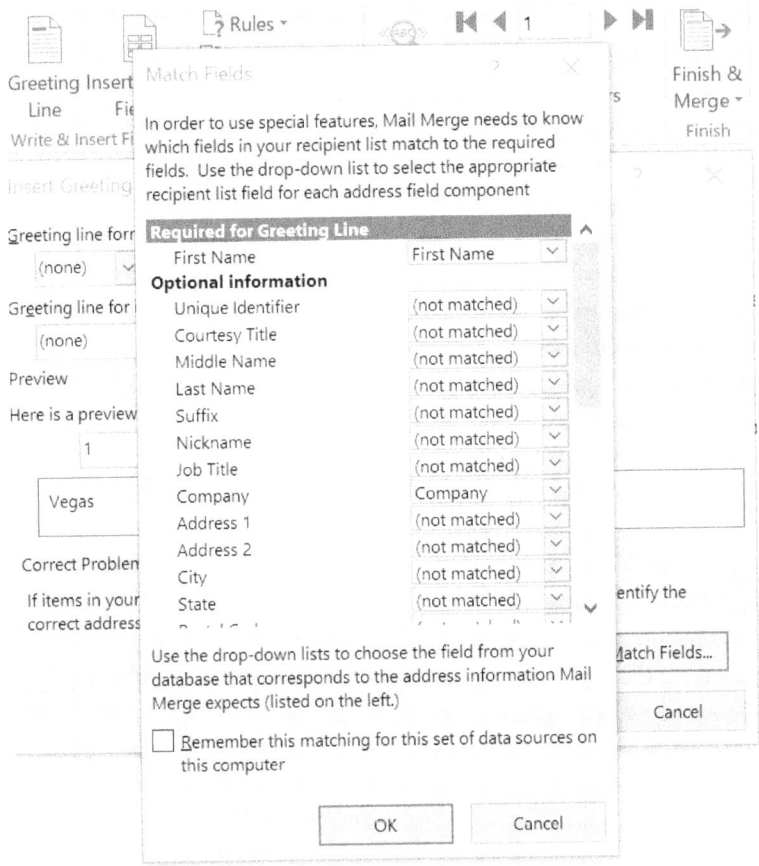

Once you hit "OK", a "Greeting Line" field will appear wherever you have your cursor, so be sure to place it next to "Name" at the top of your template. This is the field that will populate each candidate name from your excel spreadsheet. Go ahead and delete the "name" text as this field will populate by itself.

Next, we need to insert a field to populate the "company" column in our spreadsheet. Make sure your cursor is by "company" on your Word template. Click "More Items" on the right-hand column. A window will pop up titled "Insert Merge Field", and you will want to select "company" and then hit "insert."

Once you have done this, close out of the window, and you will see that a "company" field has populated where you had your cursor. Delete the company text next to the field as this field will populate each candidate's company per the column in the spreadsheet. Now that we have our email populated with the correct fields, we will move on to Step 4.

Step 4: On the bottom right of the screen (Step 4 of 6), click "Next: Preview your email message".

Once you hit preview, you will see that your email template will be populated with the first candidate's name and company information. In the top right column, you can click through each one of your recipients to preview how each email will look and assure the information has populated correctly before moving on to the next step.

Step 5: On the bottom right of the screen (Step 5 of 6), click "Next: Complete the merge".

You will then click "Electronic Mail" under the Mail Merge tab on the right side. A window will pop up with message options which should look as follows:

To: Email

Subject Line: Input your own email subject line that will appear on all emails sent to candidates

Mail format: HTML

Send records: ALL

BEWARE – Once you hit "OK", the emails will begin to send, so make sure everything is how you want before you hit the OK button!

Step 6: All Done! Go to our Outlook account to see the emails all sent. ☺

Tips for Success
As with any new tool or feature, it may take some playing around with mail merge to get it perfect and to understand all you can do with it. The best place to start is by typing up a template, or perhaps just grabbing a version of an email you recently sent, and then playing around with your data file to see all the placeholders you can come up with.

As a recruiter, you can easily populate a data file automatically by using the information you already scraped from LinkedIn and other websites about your candidates. For instance, beyond their name, you might put in details about the company they work for, their current title, where they went to school, and so on.

Once you have your two files created, go ahead and see how mail merge works. To save you time, it even gives you a "preview" option before prompted to generate all the personalized versions, so make use of that to avoid errors.

How to Create Recruiting Email Drip Campaigns

Creating email drip campaigns is an important factor within recruiting. Recruiters have been recognizing its importance copying the concept from the sales industry. The sales industry has innovated this concept and slowly improved it within the past few years. Recruiters can now fully automate an email sequence when prospecting and engaging a new candidate. There are many sales / marketing software companies that have perfected drip campaigns. Below, I will highlight the importance and how to step up a sequence using the top email tools available.

I once had the opportunity to get interviewed by Hung Lee on the Recruiting Brainfood show. During the show, we discussed the importance of email drip campaigns. Something that we both agreed on was the fact that most passive talent responds best over an email. The best way to initially engage someone new is over an email introduction. Email has become the best touch point to engage, network, and connect with potential candidates online.

What is an Email Drip Campaign?
The concept of a drip campaign is actually quite simple. In this instance, we're talking about email marketing, where a drip campaign delivers a sequence of messages at certain, pre-specified points in time to help boost engagement and clicks. Recruiters can use these tools to send out scheduled emails and follow-ups in order to attract and engage a lead.

Drip campaigns are considered more effective than the traditional (Mail Merge) email blasts that recruiters have been sending for years now. That's because drip campaigns enable you to get super personal, targeting specific prospects right in their inbox at just the right time.

When it comes to drip campaigns, response and click rates are the number one way to measure success and truly the only metrics that matter the most. An engagement from the recipient truly means that your sequence campaign has successfully worked.

Constructing an Effective Email Sequence

Constructing an effective sequence happens by trial and error. You will need to slowly experiment on a sequence to see what works and make improvements along the way. Your email should consist of the following components:

Subject Line(s): This is the line your recipient will see before they even open your email. It drives their split-second decisions to read or ignore it.

Connection: The first line in the email is what should grab them to finish reading, so they don't bounce back to their inbox. It should immediately connect to the subject line that got them to open the email. If you sound like an automated robot, odds are your email will get sent to junk.

Question: Once you have established a connection, ask a question. Be clear and upfront. If you have an open position, just say it. Be precise about what you have and create urgency by asking for a response in the next 2-3 days. Make them seem valued and that you need a response from them as soon as possible.

Email Engagement: Once the lead responses, do you have additional follow up email templates to address questions or concerns? Also, whichever tool you choose will be a factor in this. Most email sequences will stop or pause if the lead responds to the direct email.

When writing your email, remember to focus on common ground to build trust. Including a sincere compliment is also very effective. Ultimately, you need to focus on personalization, which you can still do even if you're marketing at scale.

For instance, if you're reaching out to more than 10 people, you can save time while still maximizing effectiveness by focusing on deeply personalizing the first email each person will receive. From there, you can let automation do more of the work for you, saving time while still making sure that the most important message – that first email that needs to elicit that first response – is as personal as possible.

Also, remember that simply including an organization or brand name doesn't mean an email has been personalized. You need to do some digging and go beyond that if you truly want the person reading your email to feel that all-important connection that tells them you have actually spent time considering them as an individual.

Choosing the Right Email Automation Tool
When it comes to what tools you should use to send your drip marketing campaigns, you have a few options thankfully. Below are my top suggestions:

1. Interseller.io
Schedule a customized sequence of emails that will be sent to a list of contacts. Emails stop sending automatically once the contact replies. Interseller connects with your Gmail, Outlook, Exchange, or IMAP server to send 1-on-1 emails to your contacts, so they land directly in their inbox.
Schedule a sequence of personalized emails that will be sent to the contact that will stop sending once the contact replies.
- Customize Follow-up Days
- Sequence Stops on Reply or Bounce
- Follow-up on Existing Thread or Start a New Thread

- Automatic Delay on Out of Office Emails

Other features include: Advantages scheduling automation, mail merge, ATS integrations, and tracking.

2. Resource.io

Powerful drip campaigns built for recruiting. Personalize and follow-up at scale with advanced email automation, click tracking and analytics. Never search for another email. Save time, increase response rates, and bring your relationships directly into your inbox. With Smart Labels and Reminders, you'll know which relationships are warmest, so you can send the perfect message at the perfect time.

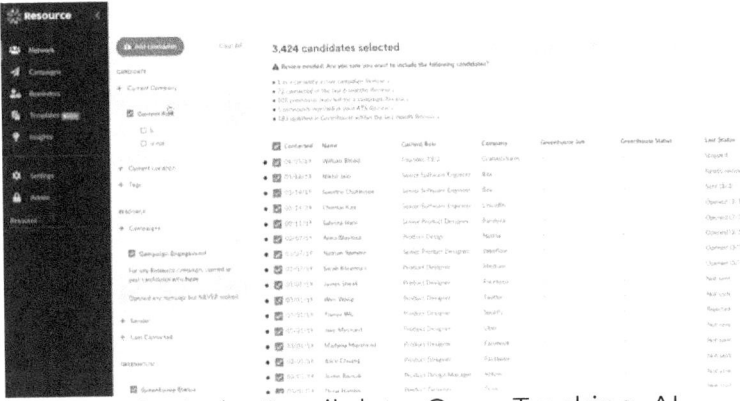

Features include: Email data, Open Tracking, AI smart follow ups, and ATS integrations.

3. Lemlist

Lemlist is the first email outreach platform that allows you to automatically generate personalized images and videos. Kickstart client relationships by making your cold emails highly personalized and human from day one. Streamline and automate your follow-ups, put repetitive tasks on autopilot and never miss a thing. Need to send emails fast and at scale without losing quality? Want to make every single email unique and personalized? Anything you need, Lemlist can handle.

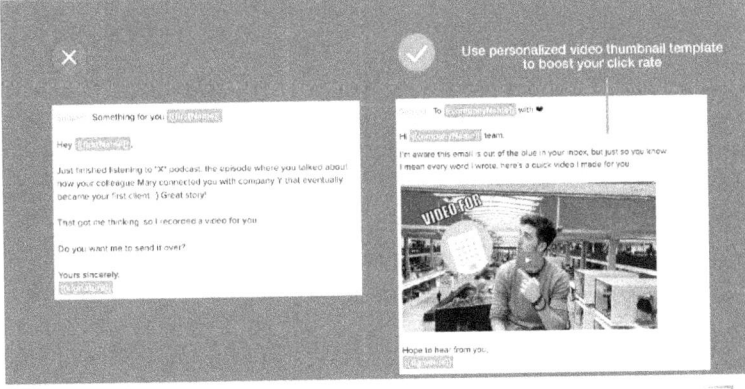

4. Gem (ZenSourcer)

Use the Chrome extension to build lists, capture candidate information, find emails, reach out, and upload to your applicant tracking system all alongside LinkedIn. More than double your response rate by sending both inmaill and automated email follow-ups. Track views, clicks, and positive replies for email and inmail to test subject lines, templates, and even time of day. Never reach out to the same person twice. Share talent maps, review candidates, and send on behalf of hiring managers.

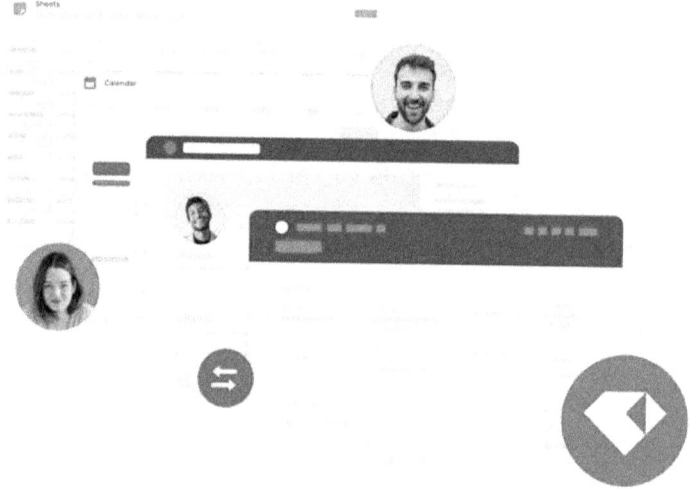

5. SeekOut

SeekOut includes the ability for recruiters to send automated multi-step email campaigns to candidates by linking their corporate email accounts with SeekOut. These emails are sent – and candidate replies are tracked – via the recruiter's corporate email address.

Now, you can take this one step further to have the emails come from your hiring manager. This feature can also be useful if you are with an RPO and use multiple corporate email addresses. This is a huge value add for recruiting teams.

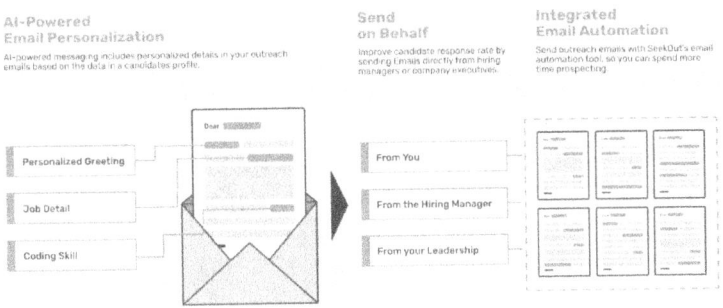

6. Hiretual (HireEZ)

Hiretual offers a variety of different tools to create email sequences automatically. Email sequence in Hiretual offers you an automatic and systematic way to engage candidates. You can build your drip campaign to 4 emails (first email + 3 follow-up emails) at the most, and the follow-up emails only send out if candidates don't reply to the previous ones.

1. Email in Bulk: Schedule and send emails to a group of candidates with one click. Personalize them by inserting email tokens (ie. first name, company) into your draft.

2. Sequence Email Templates: Create and share sequence email templates by inserting single emails to help you personalize and schedule up to 10 touch-points (This is a huge plus).

3. Engagement Insights: Receive live tips and information on predicted email performance as you type your emails or insert templates!

4. Email Delegation: Maximize the impact of your emails by sending them on behalf of a team member or hiring manager.
In either case, the right integrations and email tool will allow you to automatically push leads into your drip campaigns, so that they can begin receiving your personalized emails at just the perfect moment. The key part is making sure that your approach to drip marketing is effective, regardless of the tool you're using.

By following some basic dos and don'ts, you should be able to achieve a highly effective campaign, and you'll finally see why sales reps have been using this strategy across industries for so many years.

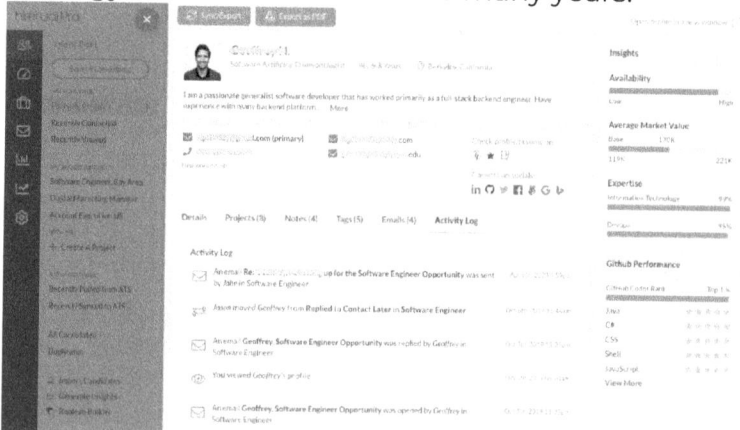

7. Trinsly

Trinsly is a tool to help successful recruiters automate parts of their job including candidate outreach and management. Send personalized emails with follow-ups in 5 seconds directly from

LinkedIn, your ATS, or any website. No more switching tabs between LinkedIn/GitHub/Stack, Gmail/Outlook, your ATS, and Excel/Spreadsheet.

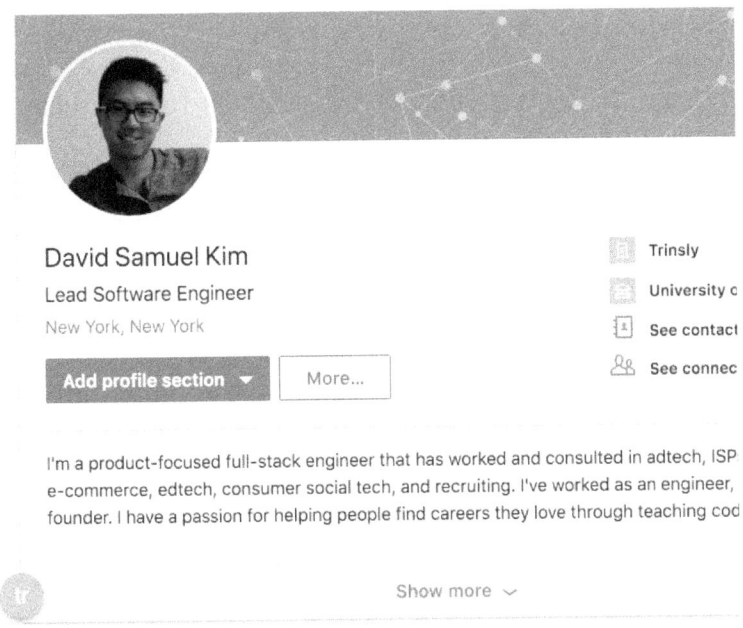

David Samuel Kim
Lead Software Engineer
New York, New York

Add profile section ▼   More...

Trinsly
University o
See contact
See connec

I'm a product-focused full-stack engineer that has worked and consulted in adtech, ISP e-commerce, edtech, consumer social tech, and recruiting. I've worked as an engineer, founder. I have a passion for helping people find careers they love through teaching cod

Show more ⌄

Example of a Full Email Sequence Template

Email Template 1:
Hi (Name),
I was impressed by your project at (Company) within this space and wanted to introduce myself. I'm a recruiter supporting our team within this (Blank) project.
I wanted to see if you would consider having a quick call to learn about our team's openings.
You can book a call below (Calendly Link)
Thanks again,
(Name)

Email Template 2:

217

Hey again (name) – I wanted to follow up from the last email yesterday about the Sys Eng role.

Have you had a chance to check out our (site) yet? Our HQ is located in [location] – great cost of living, good schools, and an amazing sense of community. Also:

We did $2.5B last year, and we've been around over 50 years – we're very stable.

We are solving some of the most interesting and cutting-edge problems across many control systems and engineering spaces – our work goes into space, foreign planets, hostile environments, etc.

We offer a flexible and collaborative environment (with unlimited PTO!!) – I know everyone says this, but we have 3,000 folks in our HQ, have far less bureaucracy than other organizations in our space, we really do care about our coworkers (happy to share real stories), and we have a really, really competitive relocation package.

Even if you're not looking, or, heavens-forbid, a Red Sox or Patriots fan (just kidding... kind of) and are not considering a move, especially to NY, let's have a chat. We'd love to at least share with you what we're doing.

We believe we're one of the best in our industry and, therefore, would relish the opportunity to connect and network with someone like you. Let me know if this is something that would be worth having a quick conversation about.

Email Template 3:
Hey (name) – Third time's the charm? I'm following up from my email 2 days ago.

Let me know if you'd consider a quick chat re: the System Engineer role with us at [company] – even if not, it'd be great to be on each other's radar!
(Name)

Email Template 4:
I'll just leave this right here...
Seriously though, Jonathan – this position needs someone who wants to be a part of creating custom, never-seen-before control systems to do things like... yes... discover life on other planets.
Let me know if this sounds like the career trajectory you're looking for. Or at least if you got a chuckle out of the meme...
(Meme Picture Included)

Note: I suggest taking a look at my other book, "The Art of the Recruiter Message," which delves deeper into the creation of personalized recruiter templates.

Finally, Review your Metrics
With these email tools you will be able to click response rates throughout the email sequence cycle. Use this metric data for your advantage to figure out what is working and also what is NOT working. Creating the perfect drip campaign will take a lot of time and effort. Keep experimenting, adjust when needed, and use trial /error to keep improving. Remember this when you get frustrated: Test, Modify, & Test Again!

Conclusion

As you become proficient in technical IT roles, you will make strides in the IT recruiting field. I am confident that this book will help take you to the next level.

I hope that it has provided you with a comprehensive understanding of major tech roles. While talent sourcing may require significant effort and work, the payoff in the long run is worthwhile.

Kindly visit my blog [WizardSourcer.com] for future updates. Furthermore, if you would be willing to write an honest review of the book on Amazon, I would be deeply appreciative. I sincerely believe that other recruiters can gain from reading this book.

Sources

The definitions related to tech competencies have been used from a variety of online sources. I've done my best to accurately write a full review of each summary section and have included my citations below:

1. Upgrade.com – Data Analyst Interview Questions
2. Guru99.com – Data Engineer Interview Questions
3. FrontEndMasters.com – Front End Handbook
4. Algrim.co – Sales Engineer Interview Questions
5. WisdomJobs.com – Data Interview Questions
6. Therootdroid.com – Devops Everything you need to know
7. Masterindatascience.com – Data Scientist
8. SprintQa.com – Devops Explained
9. Toptal.com – iOS and Android Mobile Interview Questions
10. Altexsoft.com – Solution Architect Role
11. EndTrance.com – AWS Explained
12. GitHub.com – Devops Exercises Blog
13. Stackify.com - .Net Developer Skills
14. Bleedbyes.in – Tools
15. Collegegrad.com – Software Engineers Defined
16. Bls.gov – Data Tools
17. Kitsonlinetrainings.com – SDE online training
18. Wschools.com – Full Stack Developer
19. Northeastern.edu – Data analyst skills
20. KornFerry.com – Data reports
21. HackerRank.com – Tech definitions

22. *Hired.com – Tech definitions*
23. *Wikipedia.com – Tech definitions*
24. *Codecademy.com – Tech definitions*